"This is an insightful, challenging, and potentially life-changing book. Though grounded in stories of shame and families, it yields valuable lessons for those addressing relationships in other social and institutional settings as well. As a bonus, comparing Dr. Dawson's appendix posters of the "Old Rules" versus her suggested "New Rules" makes for a brilliant little self-counseling session, all wrapped up in a bow."

David C. Yamada
Professor of Law and Director, New Workplace Institute
Co-Director, Labor and Employment Law Concentration
Suffolk University Law School

LIFE BEYOND SHAME: REWRITING THE RULES

CONNIE DAWSON PH.D.

BALBOA.
PRESS
A DIVISION OF HAY HOUSE

Balboa Press books may be ordered through booksellers or by contacting:

Balboa Press
A Division of Hay House
1663 Liberty Drive
Bloomington, IN 47403
www.balboapress.com
1 (877) 407-4847

Because of the dynamic nature of the Internet, any web addresses or links contained in this book may have changed since publication and may no longer be valid. The views expressed in this work are solely those of the author and do not necessarily reflect the views of the publisher, and the publisher hereby disclaims any responsibility for them.

The author of this book does not dispense medical advice or prescribe the use of any technique as a form of treatment for physical, emotional, or medical problems without the advice of a physician, either directly or indirectly. The intent of the author is only to offer information of a general nature to help you in your quest for emotional and spiritual well-being. In the event you use any of the information in this book for yourself, which is your constitutional right, the author and the publisher assume no responsibility for your actions.

Any people depicted in stock imagery provided by Thinkstock are models, and such images are being used for illustrative purposes only. Certain stock imagery © Thinkstock.

Print information available on the last page.

ISBN: 978-1-5043-4460-9 (sc)
ISBN: 978-1-5043-4462-3 (hc)
ISBN: 978-1-5043-4461-6 (e)

Library of Congress Control Number: 2015918703

Balboa Press rev. date: 3/18/2016

CONTENTS

*Dedicated to the worldwide members of the
Human Dignity and Humiliation Studies Network,
especially founder Evelin Lindner, M.D., Ph.D.,
and directors Linda Hartling Ph.D.
and Donald C. Klein Ph.D.*

A STORY WE CAN TELL OURSELVES

I don't believe we are born defective. I believe our perceived defectiveness is learned. The voices of shame say we should be something we're not or that we are something we shouldn't be.

When we are born, each of us brings a Light into the world and each of us comes into Being with the expectation we will be well cared for and kept safe. Call this an eternal promise. Our deepest need at this vulnerable place is to be connected to someone we can trust.

Along with joy and goodness, we encounter the challenges of unfortunate and unplanned circumstances. Being born to highly stressed parents during bombing attacks on London. Being born to a mother who dies in childbirth. Being born to a struggling family during hard economic times. Coming of age when a father is fighting a war far from home. Arriving on this Earth to parents who are in the throes of drug addiction.

From our beginnings, each of us experiences what is there for us to experience. Some experiences attract us for what they mean to our nourishment and security. Other experiences are unwelcome because they cause pain and teach us to be wary of the love and connection we crave.

Each soul is here to find its own true nature and, in the

process, enrich itself and others. Sustained by the Light and what gifts we are given, we adapt. We find any way open to us to be safe in the shadow of fearful experiences and do whatever we can to guard our Light from being extinguished. We do the best we can to belong and stay connected and alive.

PREFACE

Unshrouding Our Light

Ever since I can remember, I've been curious about how things work. *I wonder what's going on. How does that happen? Why is it that way?*

Over 30 years ago I heard Dr. Marilyn Mason, then of the St. Paul Family Therapy Institute in Minnesota[1] speak about seven rules that characterized shame-based families. My curiosity obsession shifted into high gear. *What on earth is she talking about? Shame-based what? Who? Not me. Not us.* Yet the dynamic created by the rules she described was instantly familiar. My curiosity stayed high. *How does that work and how will I know it when I see it? Could this be why I get in my own way when I want something better?*

I began by watching others, particularly noticing the one-upmanship, the manipulations, and the cut-offs between people who seemed to have reasons to be connected. I saw people connecting through conflict and ending up with resentment and separation. From a distance it looked ridiculous. People were, seemingly without consciousness, working against their own best interests. But after lots of noticing, I found that their ways and their relationship games were also mine.

Much later, as a counselor educator, as an attachment-oriented therapist specializing in working with adoptive families, and as a lecturer and co-author of several parenting books, I witnessed the shame rules in toxic action over and over again.

I delved into my own history of shame and shaming experiences, working through long-buried feelings and thoughts, looking for the keystone that holds up the shame bridge.

I defied my family rule, *Do It Yourself*, and sought help. I recognized the harm I may have caused others and made apologies where I could. I realized a need for practicing forgiveness, not only of others, but of myself. What I now call mistakes are not all in the past. Life continues to present opportunities to see shame and shaming for what it is. Better yet, the chances to practice honest and non-shaming ways to be in relationship with myself and others keep showing up. If I'm lucky, I'll get to keep replacing shame with pride as I get on with my life.

What is shameful to me is not necessarily shameful to you. Although shame is, as near as I can tell, an almost universal experience, the personal meanings we make of those experiences are uniquely our own. The seven rules, in any case, are the rules we've been taught and the ones we live by. They stand behind our experiences and they tend to have a negative impact on how we see ourselves and on our ability to participate in safe, nourishing relationships for a lifetime, unless we intentionally make the effort to change them. That's what this book is about.

Love is in the doing of it.

Anonymous

CHAPTER ONE

INTRODUCTION

I am not bound to win but I am bound to be true;
I am not bound to succeed but I am bound
to live up to what light I have.

Abraham Lincoln

Years ago I was visiting friends who lived thirty or so miles from the southern California coast. I looked to the west one morning and saw a nasty, deep greenish-brown layer between earth and sky that stretched over where Los Angeles could be. With a mix of shock and amazement, I blurted out, "Look over there!"

"Oh, yeah." My host seemed singularly unconcerned. "Looks bad today. But today is a good day. It's not so good when you can't see it, because then you know you're in it."

This book is about something as toxic as smog. It's a colorless, shapeless shroud that covers our eyes and holds us back from seeing what we see and knowing what we know. A murky layer that has a way of binding us up and keeping us from becoming the persons we were created to be.

What is this shroud? It's a set of rules based on shame that are common to most of us and largely determine what we believe about ourselves. As if that weren't enough, these rules govern how we interact in most, if not all, our relationships. These rules invite us to be fearful of being excluded at any moment, afraid we aren't good enough. And they invite us to fear being loved.

Darkness cannot drive out darkness: only light can do that.
Hate cannot drive out hate: only love can do that.

Martin Luther King, Jr.

These shame rules are anchored by our learned, internalized sense of shame. This sense has us feeling so uncertain about who we are that we become outer-focused, that is, looking outside of ourselves for clues as to how we can be okay. *What will my spouse think? What will my boss think? What will the neighbors think?* Those of us who grew up amidst the shame-based rules are hugely vulnerable to being manipulated. Why? Because we've learned we shouldn't trust ourselves.

I heard or read a definition of shame a long time ago and haven't been able to find it written anywhere since. Attributed to philosopher Jean Paul Sartre, this short and salient definition of shame makes the most sense to me. *Shame is the Self looking at the Self and finding that Self defective.*

In this book, the words *shame* and *humiliation* are used interchangeably. However, it is possible to draw a distinction between the two. Shame is largely an individually-felt and privately-held belief that there's something wrong with one's core self. Shame is associated with personal feelings of not-enoughness, failure, inadequacy, wrongness, badness. I have used the word *shame* as both a noun and a verb. *His shame was unearned* or *He was shamed unmerifully.*

Humiliation, on the other hand, can be thought of as putting individuals or groups of people in a lesser place, or "in the dirt." Humiliation works better if the person or group being humiliated already believes in their defectiveness.

Humiliation, then, is a word used to signal a strategy that has one person or group getting their needs met at the expense of another person or group by impugning their worth and dignity as human beings.

Nevertheless, shame seems to be one's personal assessment of one's very being as faulty. Imperfect. Incomplete. These findings have a way of making us feel uncertain and insecure. We think if we make a mistake, others will see our defectiveness. The Other, all Others, will see we're not good enough. Even when we are trying hard to *be* right and *do* right, we seem, somehow, to fall short. "Shame on me." So we try to fit in where we can and do the best we can.[2]

In many families, the rules that guide the relationships in the family are themselves, supposed to remain secret. They are not to be named, discussed, or negotiated. Therefore, they are never posted on refrigerators or bulletin boards for all to see. They are implicit, covert, and powerful. As such, they can be changed on a dime when it suits whoever's in charge. Keeping the rules "unknown" and fluid is a way for a family member or boss who wants the upper hand to maintain it.

How is it that we don't recognize the toxic effects of the rules? Because we've been marinating in them all the time we've existed. I have not met many families where the rules aren't unintentionally in effect. I say *unintentionally* because the rules are passed from one generation to another. **They are as natural to us as breathing.**

This doesn't stop with our families. As we move into the wider world, we take our assumptions and boundaries set by the rules with us to school, to the workplace, into politics and into other institutions in our cultures. We are only human, after all. *We do what we know.*

This book is intended to be more practical than theoretical. Knowing how to recognize shame in action is the first thing. Who wants to describe the river of sludge in which we float without some ways to get to the shore? There's a whole lot of that in this book. In fact, making the shift to new rules isn't nearly as hard as living by the old ones. There's nothing quite like the feeling of personal power we can find on the firm footing of the shore. And nothing to replace the pride of getting there.

The first chapter is devoted to thinking about how a system of rules works. The second chapter presents a way to think and talk about shame as it applies to everyday life. Both chapters lay a foundation for understanding why the shame rules work the way they do. Here's what you'll find in the next seven rules chapters:

What?	The meaning of the rule in a system based on shame
So what?	The effects of the rule on self-esteem and relationships

Now what?   Tips for putting a non-shaming new rule into practice

The stories throughout the book are true or based on true stories told to me.

The ending chapters encourage us to put our feet on a shame-free path.

I'm hoping you're ready to remove the shroud that may imprison you in so many ways. I'm hoping this may be just the right time to take a good long look at the shame-based rules to see how they are, or are not, working to help you create the best life you can. I'm hoping we're *all* ready to experience joy and pride more genuinely and deeply.

Allow beauty to shatter you regularly. The loveliest people are the ones who have been burnt and broken and torn at the seams, yet still send their open hearts into the world to mend with love again, and again, and again. You must allow yourself to feel your life while you're in it.

Victoria Erikson

CHAPTER TWO

BEGINNING WITH THE RULES

First things first.

Know the rules so you may break them properly.

Dalai Lama

The seven shame-based rules have been around for a very long time. They were developed over thousands of years and may have been necessary in the beginning to keep people safe. A lot has changed in the past few centuries and the rules have outworn their usefulness. Contemporary cultures lean more toward valuing equality and respect in relationships rather than maintaining unquestioned allegiance to a leader who promises to provide safety.

Shame rules seem to predominate in cultures where control and power over others is of higher value than the people themselves. In fact, there's a long history of using shame to gain control over others. For instance, a culture of rule by personal attack (bullying in its many forms) is meant to coerce compliance to the will of others by means of humiliation. *I'm better, you're worse. I know and you don't. I win, you lose. I am powerful, you are not.*

In brief, the seven rules are:

One: *Do and be right.* It's a good goal, but is it possible for a human being to be perfect? To never make mistakes? No. Rigid adherence to this primary rule **excludes most learning**.

Two: *Blame.* If you are found to have made a mistake or failed to live up to being perfect, move the spotlight elsewhere so your peerceived defectiveness won't be seen.

Three*: Ignore feelings.* A person would have to be dead–or deadened in order not to feel. Feelings can be denied but they never go away. Not acknowledging their information is tantamount to overriding the best survival mechanism ever devised.

Four: *Keep secrets.* Withholding information or lying throws suspicion and uncertainty into human relationships. Secrets foster separation, not connection. Secrets eat away at self-respect.

Five: *Be unclear and unaccountable.* Who recommends not being accountable and not expecting accountability from others? It's stressful and inhumane to have to live with others you can't count on. And it's disrespectful and even life-threatening to not be accountable for the agreements we've made.

Six: *Be in control.* Being in control is perhaps life's most basic survival issue we're called upon to negotiate. We must find ways to be in control of getting what we need. Being desperate for control is usually based on the fear of not having any. The control dilemma: there's a lot in life that is beyond our ability to control.

Seven: *Deny reality.* This is the *coup de grâce*, the final insult. It distorts whatever is true in our realities. It makes us feel crazy by telling us that red is blue and doing it so convincingly that we think the other might be right! It makes us forever question ourselves. Denial of reality is the essence of confusion.

All these rules are inhumane because they can't possibly be carried out without causing damage to human beings. From now on, I will refer to them as the Old Rules.

The Power of a System

The power of the rules lies in the way they work *together* to govern the interactions we have with one another. A *system* is composed of connected and interacting parts. A system as a *whole* cannot be understood by looking at a single part.[3] What might look like an impossible system of rules to figure out, actually isn't once we can see the parts (each rule) for what it is. Each rule works in concert with the others. Here's an example.

Bright and capable college student Terry earns an F in English for not turning in the major paper for the semester. Wanting to hide this fact, even from himself, he finds a way to blame his poor judgment or failure on absolutely anyone or anything. "The computer ate my course outline." "I've been so busy and that instructor expects too much." But one thing affects another. Terry doesn't tell a soul about his grade. He's afraid someone will expose his secret, which someone does, "forcing" Terry into lying more.

Terry regrets getting himself in this position. We can all finish Terry's story, including the impact on his sense of accountability, the twists and turns he made in his effort to control the situation, and the effort it took to keep denying what *really* might be going on, which loops back to why he didn't get the paper done in the first place.

The point of the story: The Old Rules are geared toward *not* solving a problem or they help protect those who fear not knowing *how* to solve a problem. They are woven together in such a way that each rule is intertwined with the others. The rules operate independently, but their interconnections augment their power. Diagnosing a problem and getting through the system to the core of it can be daunting, because each rule is so crucially enmeshed with the others.

There's an interesting feature about a system of parts. Given that each part contributes to and supports the system, changing even one part tends to throw the carefully balanced system *out* of balance. Out of balance, that is, until the system's parts have time to re-balance themselves, for the rule system, like a family system, strives for some kind of stability.

If Terry were to take responsibility for his grade, he wouldn't need to lie to himself. If he took control where he had it, blaming would be unnecessary. If he were to replace hiding his grade with being truthful about it, he might feel a sense of personal power. Taking any one of these options would result in shifting the whole situation.

The Pervasiveness of the Old Rules

There aren't many among us who haven't also experienced the negative consequences of the shame rules system, yet we seem bound to live within them, to one degree or another. Why? It's what is natural to us, because we grew up learning these rules in our families. It is there that we develop our identities and learn how to relate to one another. We take that learning and our expectations of what life holds for us into our subsequent relationships. The family is the vehicle for the transmission of these cultural norms from one generation to the next.

Our parents meant us no harm. They learned the rules in their families, and so on, back for who knows how long. Nevertheless, the shame-based rules have become a plank in the floor of our understanding about how relationships are supposed to work.

It is inevitable that we would learn to play by the rules for they are not only taught by parents. Teachers, employers, and just about everyone else uses them, too. They meant us no harm either. They were all just passing on the rules they learned from their parents, teachers, employers, and just about everyone else. We're all in this game, and most of us play by rote, because everyone else is playing by rote, too.

What Rules are Supposed to Do

Consider the purpose of rules. Rules provide for safety. Rules guide behavior. Rules and laws are meant to keep life and lives from descending into chaos and cruelty. Road rules, tax rules, property rules, employment rules, moral rules. All are written down somewhere–in constitutions and contracts, in the Bible or Quran, in manuals and codes.

Rules literally draw the line. They define the boundaries between what's helpful and what's hurtful. When they're clear and written down, they can be put on the table for discussion, where they can be re-negotiated if they aren't working to keep people safe and life fair–or as fair as possible.

We each decide when we'll get out of bed in the morning. That's a personal rule that puts a boundary on our activity. Maybe we prefer eating protein for breakfast and avoiding a gooey caramel roll, so even though we'd love the roll, we eat eggs. That's a rule, or boundary, we've set based on what we believe is good for us and not good for us. Here's another example for yourselves: What line have you drawn about being at work on time? Is it okay to be 10 minutes late? Is it *not* okay to be 15 minutes late? Is it good for you to be late at all? You draw boundaries all the time. The boundaries are your personal rules and form a container within and from which you conduct life's business. Rules are inevitably made for protection and safety.

Out of understanding comes every form of love.

Sherwin Newland

11

Chapter Three

WHAT'S SHAME GOT TO DO WITH IT?

The divine music is incessantly going on within ourselves,
but the loud senses drown the delicate music,
which is unlike and infinitely superior to anything
we can perceive with the senses.

Mahatma Gandhi

Because we unconsciously and fiercely defend our shame from being seen by others, we do all we can to defend ourselves from exposure. As noted earlier, Sartre described shame as "the Self looking at the Self and finding that Self defective." And we don't want anyone else to see that defectiveness. We believe that whatever it is that's *wrong* or that isn't *right* with us, if seen, will cause others to run the other way.

It is that part in each of us that we don't want anyone to know, the part we believe is shameful, which enables the Old

Rules system to work. By hooking the shame we carry, others can control us, for shame has a way of shutting people down. We are thus vulnerable to being manipulated or coerced into situations and into being with people who aren't good for our mental and physical health.What does shame look like? The classic physical *look* of shame is droopiness, head down, eyes averted, appearing to be vacant, frozen. But there's so much more. There are the defenses we use to keep from being *seen* as defective.

Rage, Contempt and Perfectionism

One response to having our shame exposed is rage, especially the rage that seems much stronger than whatever triggered it. This rage is sometimes camouflaged and sometimes not. The rage is intended to have others keep their distance. *Don't tread on me! Don't see (what I fear is) the real me. I am bad. Don't touch me!*

Still others may respond to exposure with contempt for the one who gets too close, who might see too much. Contempt is when we literally turn away from being seen. *I will turn my back on you. You are inferior and not worth my time. I will turn away from you. You are not important to me.* Contempt is a harsh and often a silent way to cut off an interaction. It's a clever, if confusing, attempt for one person to offload the unwanted part of herself onto another person, thereby blaming the other person for the cut-off. *It's your fault I'll have nothing to do with you. You're not worth my attention.* Meaning *emotional distance is my friend.*

Perhaps the most common defense we use to protect ourselves from being seen is the drive to be perfect. *I'll prove to one and all that I'm okay (not defective) by not making any mistakes. If I make a mistake, I might as well erect a billboard to my wrongness or insufficiency.* Every potential "mistake" becomes a risk. Limiting creativity and stopping short of success are two of the hallmarks of perfectionism.

Let's just agree that no one rushes to the head of the line anxious to declare, *Look at me! I'm defective!* The experience of being exposed as "wrong" makes us want to hide. The feelings can be so overwhelming, our brains can't think of anything *but* hiding, or better yet, disappearing.

We fear being tagged as unworthy, unacceptable, or unwanted if others see our faultiness. We don't exist in a vacuum. We need others to survive, so we strive to keep ourselves in the most favorable light possible. We need to belong, since we don't do well if we are not connected to others. This is a big motivator to comply with what others want and to hide our perceived defectiveness any way we can.

Shame or Guilt?

The words *shame* and *guilt* are often used interchangeably, but their meaning is different. Shame is about our defectiveness. Guilt is about having engaged in behavior that violates values we hold.

Guilt bells go off when we're behaving outside of what we perceive to be our integrity. Guilt bells clang when I don't visit my ailing mother as often as I think I should. Guilt bells clang when I deny saying what I said to others about my best friend. When I'm not proud of how I behaved, I feel off-balance. Outside of my integrity. Guilty.

When our behaviors and values don't match, changing either our behavior or our values will quiet our guilt. I can visit my mother as often as I intend *or* change my intention about how often I will make those visits. I can tell my friend the truth, repair any damage done, and act according to my value of being honest and kind. It is totally within my power to get back into balance by paying attention to my feelings of guilt.

I also have the option of changing my values to match my behavior. I will make visits to my mother at my convenience. The relationship with my friend is wearing down and is no longer important. Either choice will relieve my guilt and I can feel congruent and back in balance.

Not so with shame. Guilt is about behavior, which I can change. Shame is about personhood. Shame means that *I, myself*, am wrong. Not just wrong. Faulty. A mistake or error in judgment on my part simply broadcasts my shame. What power do I have to bring myself into balance if I am defective? *I am not* doesn't counter *You are stupid.* How do I *prove* I'm not defective without appearing to be just that?

Telling the difference between shame and guilt starts with getting the lay of the proverbial land to gather relevant data. In the case of shame, looking at our histories will provide some clues. What have we learned that has us believing we are unworthy or defective? How did we come to believe that we had to hide or protect ourselves from exposure if we made a mistake?

Whether the feelings are of guilt or shame, both indicate the existence of a problem to solve. The great thing about guilt is that when we've screwed up, we can admit our wrongdoing, take resposibility for our part of what happened, and go on to make amends for the harm we may have done. This is why our goal will be to take better care of ourselves by turning shame feelings into feelings of guilt. More about that as we go on.

Possible Origins of Shame

Many professionals and researchers have tackled the question of how shame gets internalized in the human psyche. However, speaking practically, when it comes to understanding shame, much depends on what we believe to start with. If we believe we are born in original sin, then shame is inherent to our being alive. We are born in shame and therefore, shameful in our essence. If we believe a sense of shame develops in infancy or early childhood when caretakers are distant or hostile, then a sense of shame originates when, as children, we assume it's our fault and conclude there must be something wrong with us. Remember, a very young child is oriented toward survival, not reasoning.

We may believe that a sense of shame begins when authority figures dismiss, disrespect, discount, and otherwise show disdain by name-calling, ridiculing, and all other means of humiliation, both public and private.[4] Or you may be familiar with the work of developmental psychologist Erik Erikson.[5] If so, you may believe that personal feelings of shame relate to how we resolve the Autonomy vs. Shame and Doubt dilemma. What decisions do we make about how personally effective and secure we are?

Any or all of these beliefs may be true. Actually, it probably isn't worth getting side-tracked by thinking we have to decide which premise is correct. Side-tracking is a common device to steer away from the real problem at hand, namely, *what can I do to deal with being shamed, with having been shamed, and with shaming others?*

How Does a Sense of Personal Shame Originate?

My personal theory is this: In spite of being hard-wired to connect with our Important People when we are born, we meet ones who are preoccupied or distracted by their own problems, or who are swamped with fear, or who lack the skills or support to respond to us in a connecting way. So we fall into these questions. *Why can't I get their attention? Maybe I'm not a good signaler of what I need. What's wrong with me?*[6]

Over time, with added insults like separation, ridicule, contempt, neglect, hurt and humiliation, the developing child comes to believe she is not deserving and not worthy, and that there must be something missing or wrong with her. Once the seeds of shame have been planted, when conditions are "right" they take root. The adaptations I make and the inferences I draw become part of who I believe myself to be–my internalized sense of shame. Conversely, a strong early belief in my level of security and "enoughness" is an inoculation against being vulnerable to shaming from individuals and situations.

Whatever shame we may carry, that shame was never intended to define who we are. The vast majority of humans don't set out to make their children feel as miserable or angry as they, themselves, felt as children. They just don't know or believe there's a better way to love them. If we've grown up thinking we are *less than* and defined ourselves as *less than*, that is definitely not who we really are. Our shame is *an early belief about ourselves* that we can change.

Think of yourself as an incandescent power, illuminated
and perhaps forever talked to by God and his messengers.

Brenda Ueland

Shame Can Support Self-Control

Shame isn't all bad. Shame has served a protective function throughout the ages by reminding members belonging to any group of the line between acceptable and unacceptable behaviors. *Put your clothes on before you go out onto the street.*

The warnings vary depending on culture, community, family, and religious norms for unacceptable behavior – anything about us we wouldn't want shouted from the rooftops. *I don't rob someone because I'm afraid of getting caught and bringing shame on my family. I don't have sex outside of marriage because my community doesn't approve of it. Fathers don't have sex with their daughters...or sons. Don't (fill in the blank).* Like a governor placed on a car controls its maximum speed, fear of humiliation or not belonging is meant to affect our behavior choices.

The threat of shame can stop us in our tracks. Given voice, the feelings say, *The behavior you are engaging in or about to engage in, is outside the bounds of what is acceptable. Stop now! You are at risk! Stay on this side of the line and be okay and one of us, or cross over the line and suffer the consequences.* Shame can serve a protective function by keeping us within the bounds of what our culture or group deems to be okay.

Shame has a lot to do with the management of human drives, chief among them, the sexual drive. The possibility of being shamed functions as a measure of control over behaviors that are seen as undermining relationships and the life of the larger group or society. Breaking the rules carries penalties, humiliations like shunning, separation, isolation from the group, and in some eras and some cultures, private or public flogging and other physical punishments.

Thus, the fear of being shamed can serve as a monitor on our impulses. There are times when the heat of the moment, or the pressures of peers or the temptation to engage in immoral or illegal behavior pulls us to the edge of our own good sense and values. It is at those times that thinking about the consequences (quite beyond the fear of getting caught) helps us consider what's good for us. If the thought is unbearable, we pull back.

High school sweethearts Harry and Suzanne lingered at the shore of the lake one early summer moonlit evening. One thing led to another. At a certain point, Harry suddenly seized Suzanne and ran into the chilly water with her in his arms. Years later, Harry said with a smile, "That pretty quickly put an end to what was about to happen."

The point? If we know the consequences of a behavior and **we don't want those consequences**, we heed the warning. Well, some do and some don't. If we know the consequences and do the behavior anyway, we're said to be out-of-control, defiant, or uncaring, when in reality, we might be rebellious or have different values.

Shame may have been *intended* to support self-control. However, shame injects a troublesome and toxic aspect into the picture when the shamer's intention is to take someone down to put themselves up, no matter what the human costs. In other words, getting their own needs met at the expense of others.

The Usefulness of Shame in Controlling Others

Shaming (humiliation) is often used to control others. Here's where the mischief begins. There are those who need others to do what *they* want them to do. They ask. They cajole. They try to convince. They manipulate. They intimidate. They demand. They warn. They threaten. They humiliate. They punish. Costs to others be darned.

For instance, soldiers of one religious belief rape the enemy army's wives and daughters to shame their opponents and gain an advantage. Using humiliating tactics to bring down an opponent has a long and tragic history. Shaming others to control them is first learned at home. *I know and you don't. I'm right and you're wrong. I'm up and you're down. This hurts, but I do this because it's what you need. This is for your own good.*

For those whose own goals are satisfied by controlling others, the Old Rules are a ready-made device that may get them what *they* need, but not necessarily what the *others* need.

Discipline teaches what to do, or what to do instead.
Punishment inflicts pain.

Unknown

Particularly in Parenting

Not many years ago, there was a widespread belief that a good parent's first and foremost job was to raise children up in the sight of God. To most, that meant to raise children perfectly so the children would be perfect. It didn't matter that there was no perfect parent! Anything a parent needed to do to get a child to conform and obey, any beating, or berating, any emotional battering was fair.

We're only a few years away from feeding infants no oftener than every four hours and showing them only limited affection. According to one parenting expert of the time, "limited" meant once a year. One wonders what the infants made of this.

A mother whose son was born in 1930 was asked how she handled the best parenting advice of the day, which was to feed her infant every four hours. Period. The mother said, "I couldn't stand it. He cried so hard, but I knew I wanted to be a good mother, so I put my coat on and walked around the block until it was time to feed him." When her son was in his 50s, she told him she was so sorry she'd done that. "It didn't seem right to me, but I listened to what I was supposed to do and not to myself."

Most parents love their children and want the best for them. How they show and transmit their love varies a lot, depending largely on the decisions they made a long time ago related to their own histories. For instance, as an act of love, a parent may humiliate her child to "get him ready" to survive in a dangerous neighborhood. It doesn't look like an act of love to an outsider, but the parent heard it from her parent and knew the intention was always to keep a beloved child alive. It was meant to be an act of caring.

There are many ways to get the love message across. "Tony, I love you and I want you to know if you do anything that jeopardizes your life, I'm coming to get you!" The words of Tony's mother still remind him of who he is and what he's about. His mom said over and over, "Tony, you are not for joining a gang. You are for going to school." And he did.

If you ever heard "shame on you," when you were a child, what did you take that to mean? "Stop what you're doing!" The words themselves, plus a certain accusatory, sharp tone of voice and a shocked, stern, angry, or disappointed facial expression leaves little room for interpretation. Children, particularly small ones, can jump to the conclusion that something's wrong with them. Although their behavior is what gave rise to "shame on you," in the absence of an explanation of why what they're doing is unacceptable, they're left to conclude that they themselves are what is unacceptable.

For parents who want a different way to stop unwanted or dangerous behavior, there are options to the automatic shaming stopper. It is the job of parents to nurture and structure children. *Nurturing* means the many ways of caring for, loving, and supporting children. *Structuring* means setting boundaries for safety and protection, teaching morals and values, and teaching all manner of skills.[7]

Experience is how life catches up with us and teaches us to love and forgive each other.

Judy Collins

Striking a More Trustworthy Balance

Putting even-handed, balanced structure and nurture together makes for powerful parenting. In order to get perspective on shame-based rules, a basic look at the helpful and not-so-helpful ways of delivering both structure and nurture may help.[8]

Structure

Parents are entitled to and expected to impose rules on their children when the children are young, because the children are not yet sufficient in knowledge and experience to make and carry through on their own rules for protection and safety. A parental rule that a small child cannot cross the street by himself is a wise one and up to the parents to teach and enforce. As they mature, however, we expect children will learn to be increasingly responsible for their own rules and safety. They must be able to cross the street safely by themselves! To do that, they need to think, to assess risks, to project consequences, and more. *What do I need? Where will I draw the line between yes and no? What is good for me and what is not?*

A parent who is a rigid rule-maker makes rules more for his benefit than the child's. Input from the child or paying attention to the child's increasing competence is not welcomed. A child doesn't have much of a chance to negotiate. Feeling unrecognized and unheard, that child tends to rebel at some point, particularly because he senses it's his job to grow up and learn how to make his own rules someday. (See the Structure Chart in Appendix A.)

On the other hand, parents who fail to make rules or fail to enforce the rules they make abandon their job. Children grow up not knowing where their edges are, not knowing what's good for them. Everyone seems to want their freedom, but when they truly have it, they or the people they affect aren't all that happy about it. Speaking of her experience as an 8-year-old child, one adult said, "I could see my parents didn't know what to do with me and somehow I instantly knew I was in trouble."

A simple way to think about making rules is this: When it's a matter of protecting children and keeping them safe, state it in the form of a **non-negotiable rule**. *Bedtime is at 7.* At some developmental point, however, it's appropriate to shift to a **negotiable rule**. *It's time to see if you're ready to have a later bedtime* is a good way to signal that the topic is open for discussion. The negotiation stops when the parent is satisfied the new bedtime continues to support the health and well-being of the child.

Nurture

Nurturing involves the ways we care for children and one another. Structure without nurture is brittle. Nurture without structure is soft, but without bones. Structure *with* nurture is strong and loving,

There are two important human needs, or hungers,[9] that nurturing satisfies: **recognition**, to be acknowledged, and **stimulation**, touch, movement and contact. (**Certainty** is the hunger for structure, the physical, social, and psychological systems that keep us safe.) Satisfying these hungers is the job of caregivers.

Nurture is unconditional. We deserve nurture because we're here. Think of the following six ways to nurture as if they were like a highway. The center positions of *Assertive Care* and *Supportive Care* provide the quality of care that best contributes to feelings of love and security. If a child or adult is unable to care for themselves and unable to ask for what they need, we think *for* them, decide what they need, and provide it. That's *Assertive Care.* The other place of clear nurture is *Supportive Care.* When someone knows what they need and is able to meet that need, we show caring by supporting them in their efforts. We can provide help if they ask for it or we can offer help, which they may accept, refuse, or negotiate.

The next adjacent two positions, similar to the shoulders of a highway, are *Conditional Care* and *Overindulgence.* They involve costs to both giver and receiver. *Conditional Care* is care that carries a pricetag. *I'll love you if you do well in school* or *I'll pay attention to you if you're on the starting five on the basketball team. Overindulgence* is giving too much and doing something for another that they are capable of doing for themselves. Neither of these positions is unconditional, taking care of another just because they exist.

As the outer positions, or ditches, are hard on cars, so are *Neglect* and *Abuse* hard on children. Neglect ignores children's needs. Neglect is the absence of care. Extreme neglect is perhaps the deepest wounding children can experience. Something, anything, even if it fails to meet any reasonable test of positive nurture is preferable to nothingness. Abuse most often includes harsh physical invasion, although emotional and intellectual invasion is frequently present as well. Why is abuse considereed nurture? Because in the absence of any better recognition, children have to use what they get as verification they are alive, even though it's toxic and painful. In a sense, they adapt to their circumstances by becoming garbage convertors.

We accept the love we think we deserve.

Stephen Chbosky

Inadvertent Shaming

Shaming may stop a dangerous or unwanted behavior, but it breaks an interpersonal bridge. If the bridge is left disconnected and hanging, the relationship is broken, or at least, cracked. Jake didn't use the *shame on you* words. He didn't need to.

Jake was mowing the lawn and looked up to see 2-year-old Buddy starting to cross the street at the same time he saw a car headed straight for his son. Jake was too far away to grab Buddy, so he screamed his son's name as forcefully and angrily as he could. "Buddy!" Buddy stopped in his tracks and froze. Then he collapsed in tears.

Jake rushed to Buddy, and in spite of Buddy's pushing him away, Jake picked him up firmly but lovingly. Buddy wouldn't look at his dad and pushed him away, even hitting him once or twice on the arm.

Jake calmed himself and Buddy by saying things like "It's okay" and "I love you, Bud" and "I was so scared. I didn't want the car to hit you."

When Jake yelled, he broke an interpersonal bridge with his son, who, as most young children do, sought to stay in his dad's good graces. Jake recognized Buddy's shame response and knew he needed to reconnect. Jake's goal was safety but Buddy didn't know that. Shaming broke the relationship bridge he and Buddy had built. By using nurturing touch and comfort and a little calming time, Jake did his part to re-build the bridge with his son.

Changing learned parent behaviors requires persistence and compassion for ourselves. Responding automatically in a way all too familiar and unwanted can remind us to ask for a do-over.

Emily and Sis were doing what 4-year-olds do. They were playing House. Emily was being Dad and Sis was playing Mom. At one point, Sis' mom overheard the girls quarreling. "Play nice with your friend, Sis," she called out.

A few minutes later, Mom heard Sis yelling at Emily. "Can't you do anything right?" Mom virtually leapt to the playroom. "Shame on you, Sis! You know better than that! Look! You made Emily cry."

After soothing Emily, Mom noticed Sis was gone. Mom found her hiding behind the toy box in her room, looking as if the stuffing had been pulled out of her. "You're okay, Sis. I'm sorry, Honey. When I heard myself, I realized I didn't like it when my mom yelled 'Shame on you' at me either and I should have known better than to yell it at you."

With a smile and outstretched arms, she said "What do you say we get in some snuggle time right now? I'd love that."

Checking for Impact

Encountering for the first time how the Old Rules and shame are connected can stop us from going further. The following ideas provide a few entry points into looking more closely at the ideas in this chapter.

- Do a shame history or a shame timeline. Include the people and situations that first come to mind. What happened? Who was involved? What was your response and what did you decide about yourself, others, and your life?
- Identify friends and family who love and respect you and will listen with their hearts and without judgment or advice as you begin disentangling the origins of the shame you may be carrying.
- Get acquainted with the Affirmations in Appendix B. You may want to ask someone you trust to read them to you. The affirmations are positive parent messages. Take them in as if you believed them, for someday soon, you will.
- For those who like to consider the bigger picture, try reading or listening to any local, national, or international situation to see if you can identify an Old Rules shame dynamic.

Moving On

The next chapters are devoted to looking for the dynamics associated with each rule. Uncovering some of these dynamics will help us see what we're seeing and understand how the system of Old Rules works. We must first know them well enough to decide what we want to keep and what we want to change. To be in a good position to make those evaluations, looking at the What, So What, and Now What of each rule can help us decide what may be good for us and what may not.

1. WHAT? What the rule says; what the rule means.
2. SO WHAT? Some effects of the rule, especially in families.
3. NOW WHAT? Naming a replacement rule with ideas for switching out of the Old Rules and into the New.

Rivers know this: there is no hurry. We shall get there some day.

A.A. Milne

CHAPTER FOUR

OLD RULE 1: DO RIGHT AND BE RIGHT

Be morally, intellectually, and socially right.
Don't make mistakes. Regard yourself and others
harshly for errors in judgment and performance.

WHAT? The Meaning of the Old Do Right and Be Right Rule

Most of us don't set out to do things wrong. Even a bank robber has a right and wrong way to rob a bank. The word *right* itself is a stumbling block to understanding this rule. *Right* can mean correct, appropriate, just, straightforward, honest, and so much more. The meaning of the word is important because we have to understand what the rule is saying before we can comply with it properly.

Ahmed left his office at 5 on the dot in hopes of catching the 5:15 subway. His haste paid off. He claimed a seat near the front of the car, one of the only seats left.

Among the crowd entering at the next stop was a middle-age woman who was barely holding herself together. In spite of getting her hand on the pole, she would have fallen if it hadn't been for the bodies crowded around her.

Ahmed stood and beckoned the distressed woman to take his seat. He couldn't tell why she was so unsteady but he and the passenger across the aisle kept an eye on her without being obvious about it. Something clearly wasn't right.

Ahmed's stop was next and he started inching his way toward the door. Lo and behold, the woman was right behind him. "Do you need help?" he asked, She shook her head no.

The doors opened and in the rush of riders leaving, Ahmed turned when he heard a collective gasp. The woman had fallen face first onto the platform with her feet in the space between the platform and the train. Ahmed and a handful of others automatically went into action.

One pulled the alarm on the train; two or three others tended to the woman, who was unable to get up and who had visible wounds that needed care; another called 911; and Ahmed went to the top of the stairs to direct the EMTs to her position. "It's as if we were a practiced team. Very few words passed between us. We reassured the woman that she would be okay, telling her help was on the way. One of the women spread her coat over the woman and one of the men rolled up his newspaper so she had a better place to put her head. We all stayed until she was safely in the care of professionals."

In telling this story, Ahmed said, smiling proudly, *"We strangers did the right thing and we couldn't have pulled it off better if we'd tried. It was a really great feeling!"*

Yes, few of us would contend that there's anything wrong with *doing the right thing.* In Ahmed's situation, people seemed to share a sense and a knowledge about what was needed, *Right* meant getting help for someone who needed it.

But what happens when two or more people disagree about what's right? Fresh food or frozen? Fluroide in the drinking water or not? Complying with the speed limit or not? Cleaning up your mess or leaving it for others? What's right? Our lives are filled with conflicts based on the *Who's right, What's right* issue. And this is just the small stuff.

What about stuff that's bigger, like differences about the right way to rear children. In this regard, several Biblical references might shed light on the meaning of *right.*

Train up a child in the way he should go, even when he is old and he will not depart from it. Proverbs 22:6

Folly is bound up in the heart of a child, but the rod of discipline drives it far from him. Proverbs 22:15

All Scripture is breathed out by God and profitable for teaching, for reproof, for correction and for training in righteousness. Timothy 3:16

Faced with agreeing, or at least deferring, on how children will be reared, each party will probably have a personal meaning for what *right parenting* means. Anyone who has experienced being a parent knows that putting together two ideas about *right* takes some doing. Deciding what's right seems so simple and it's anything but.

What's Right? Who's Right?

Since being right is paramount to the way the first shame system rule functions, we'll stop to get clearer about what the rule means and how it holds the shame-based rules together. If we assume the first rule is unassailable because we all aim to do what is right, we might miss why it's first on the list of shame-based rules.

Try applying the *RIGHT* test to everyday examples.

> What's the right way to make coffee?
> What's the right way to please a boss?
> What's the right way to teach a child not to hit his little brother?
> What's the right position on gun control?
> What's the right religion? The right political party? The right skin color?
> The right school? The right marriage partner?

Does *right* mean to do the correct thing? If so, correct according to whom?

Do the moral thing? Moral according to whom? Do the accepted thing? Accepted according to whom?

You have probably already gathered that there are at least several, and often many right ways to do almost anything. There are always some absolutes; there's a right way to turn on your computer, make a left turn and so on. Life would be simple if there were always one right way to do most of what we do, for we would be relieved of the burden of making choices. Eventually though, chances are we'd feel a push to burst out of the narrowness of a world with so few options and so little room for creativity, self-expression, exploration, and so on.

We might simply explain the first rule of *Do and be right* by stating it according to what it most often means: DO IT MY WAY.

Our parents' right way was theirs, even though it may not have felt so good to us and didn't even seem to work out well for them. Nonetheless, **this rule implies that we should not make mistakes**. But it's human to make mistakes. Mistakes are for learning about life and ourselves. We do the best we know how and when we see an unwanted outcome, we find out what to do differently and change so we don't have to continue to make the same mistakes.

The reality is this. There's almost always more than one way to do just about anything and more than one way to do it so that it harms the least and helps the most.

Those who take absolute RIGHT/WRONG positions have to disqualify anything that doesn't fit their boxed-in frame of right and wrong. These disqualifications are at the heart of most problems because we begin to drift into fooling ourselves about what is real. Acknowleging and solving problems requires discriminating between what is true and what is not.

For example, Ashley believes in being celibate before marriage. So does her very best friend, but when this friend delivers a baby five months after her wedding day, Ashley *seems* to believe it is possible to give birth to a 9 pound baby after a five-month pregnancy. She disqualifies reality to save herself from having to face the facts. No wonder! Having to decide if her friend was right (or wrong) would mean she might have to choose between her beliefs, her friend, and the facts as she believed them to be.

Some Truth About RIGHT

An old friend of mine began to reflect on her history of learning the rule about doing and being right. This is Emma's story.

I spent several years in therapy finding my parents wrong about many things. The truth is, they weren't perfect but they taught me any number of skills and values that have worked well for me. They taught me not to steal. They taught me that if I harmed another person by stealing, I had to face the person and make restitution. They taught me to put myself in the shoes of others. They taught me all kinds of skills that have served me well, like how to live within a budget, how to drive a stick-shift, and how to put a dinner on the table.

There were other things they taught me, intentionally and unintentionally. Things like what I thought I did, and didn't, deserve in a relationship and how to be nice and not stick up for myself.

I grew up confused about the discrepancy between what my parents said about our family and my experience of being in it. "We are a happy family," they said.

"Your family is a happy family," others in the town said. Yet it often didn't feel that way.

I decided my parents and the others must be right and I must be wrong. I don't remember giving voice to the part of me that screamed, "This can't be right!" I went along in order to belong. And I kept my distance to be emotionally safe.

As a child, I couldn't see there might be a difference between what was right for my parents and what was right for me, and when I married, I recreated the unspoken rules of their relationship. For instance, when I recognized the bumpy spots and impasses in my marriage, I didn't insist on getting outside help. Need I mention my parents would never have sought help?"

We all tend to be more comfortable with what is familiar than what is unknown and unpredictable so it's automatic to do what's familiar.

Do it right messages from those who love us come through in many verbal and nonverbal ways. Emma recounted her mother's advice. *It's no use going to counseling to fix your marriage. Life will be too hard if you don't get along with what you've got. And remember, divorce is hard on children. He's not perfect, but you'll be fine.* The advice was rooted in how her mother handled problems in her marriage. Emma wished she had instead heard something like "If your husband won't see a counselor with you, go by yourself to see if you can figure out why you are unhappy. Get the help you need to decide what you can change and what's best for you and your family.

It's our job to know what's right for *us*. In the process of sorting that out, coming to understand ourselves couldn't be more important. It helps if we stay conscious of who and what is going on around us. Is that something I want or is it unwanted? To what do I say YES and to what do I say NO? Being aware of the emotional impact of our everyday experiences is central to discovering the selves we may be only superficially acquainted with. We are the experts of who we are and what we need. We are the experts of ourselves. We are the ones who must let ourselves know our intentions. Identifying who we are and what we need is not a job to turn over to others, for that means they are in control of us and we are not.

In order to learn more in a shorter period of time, Emma found a therapist. She had avoided getting help for a long time and finally had to admit she hadn't thought she could handle what she might find out about herself. That turned out to be another of her erroneous beliefs!

SO WHAT? Some Effects of Do and Be Right in the Family

How does the unacknowledged presence of the Do and Be Right rule have a long-term effect on family members? This list is a beginning. Add what you yourself have observed or experienced.

- Children hear and internalize chronic criticism through name-calling (Dummy, Stupid, Slut) or comments (You don't have the brains you were born with...). They also hear themselves programmed to lose (You never..., you always...).
- Children develop self-concepts that are skewed. Early messages are delivered by adults who have themselves been schooled in the art of judging others. If behavior falls short, judgment is made against the person, NOT the behavior. There's no offer of help toward making children more skillful, and thus, more confident. (With your grades, what makes you think you're college material?)
- Children develop defenses to keep others from seeing how inadequate they feel inside. (Estella reflexively

makes excuses even when she doesn't have to. Sammy finds fault with everybody and everything.)

- Relationships are contaminated because no one is immune from being seen as defective or being regarded as less than they *are*. (Family members focus on things like blaming others, trading insults, and avoiding one another.)

- Family members yearning to be closer feel too unsafe to risk verbal intimacy.

- Communication is distorted through word, touch, and deed.

- Family members don't recognize when a problem is a problem and avoid solving the problems they do recognize.

- Family members feel unsafe.

- Trust is always an issue.

As I said in the Introduction, the Do and Be Right rule is not posted on the refrigerator. It is implicit. As such, it is unassailable, not subject to negotiation. It's like a secret that everyone knows and does not express. To actually address it in a family so steeped in a don't-make-mistakes mentality is unthinkable, or at the very least, it can make the secret-breaker a target in a system that doesn't welcome change.

Battles About What's Right

The rule about doing and being right inevitably spawns antagonism in relationships.

Harry and Sally discovered they had very different opinions about disciplining their children. Harry tended to have "the talk" pointing out the positive and negative effects of his children's behavior choices. He was, at heart, a teacher, and he believed that his children were reasonable and would see the wisdom of his counsel. Sally, on the other hand, believed that good fences made good neighbors, and that children exceeding carefully drawn limits needed to feel the consequences of their actions, painful though they might be. In their disagreement, it wasn't long before Mom and Dad began trading criticisms, blaming one another and arguing about who was right.

Sally's anger about their disagreements finally burst through. "I don't like how I'm resenting you, Harry! We'd better get this figured out, fast!"

Where winning is paramount, getting into control battles results in increased distance between the parties and on top of that, the conflict remains unresolved! Too often, the next step is capitulation, more separation, or escalation and violence. Conflicts can and should lead to greater understanding and deeper trust. In order to ride the boat successfully through conflict's waters, it takes listening with great heart to another's thoughts and feelings. It's during these times we discover our common beliefs and can work from there to come together. That is what happens when conflicts are addressed and resolved with mutual respect, compassionate listening and the humility to drop the defensiveness of *my way or else.*

Harry and Sally agreed that at least one clearheaded third party should help them sort out a way of disciplining that met their shared goal– raising responsible and loving children. The first new rule of their negotiations was this: We maintain mutual respect. The second was this: We agree to do our best to understand one another's beliefs, fears, hopes, and experiences. And the third rule was: When we reach an agreement, we will support one another in implementing it.

Beyond what control battles do to relationships, most parents know that when Mom and Dad have differing beliefs about something as important as discipline, the creative child tends to take advantage by exceeding boundaries that are set for her security. This is one of the ways children become collateral damage to the *Who's Right?* wars of the parents.

———————

Listening is so close to being loved that most people can't tell the difference.

David Augsberger

———————

The Four Culprits

When a learned sense of shame has us believing there must be something wrong with who we are, we absolutely don't want anyone to notice or otherwise call attention to our faults. Keep that spotlight away! Put it somewhere else!

There are four strategies, four *culprits*, most commonly used to deflect the Do and Be My Way spotlight. Being able to name them helps us know what's going on when we're on the receiving end and can help us identify when we're using them.

These four culprits have been around for eons and facilitate the operation of shame-based rules:

1. Thinking primarily of behaviors and people in terms of right/wrong, good/bad, either/or, win/lose
2. Being hypocritical
3. Being confused and confusing by giving mixed messages
4. Being judgmental

As much as these can defend the imperfect Self we want to hide, they are also used to gain control or establish superiority over others. We may use them to hide, or they may be used by others who are hiding and want us to be confused about who is responsible for what.

In the spirit of "it takes one to know one," identifying how *others* use these defensive maneuvers can be a clue that the shadow of shame is present. If we find ourselves using one of the culprits, that may be a clue to us to step out of a situation and take time to review what's happening. Why am I feeling defensive here? What's going on?

Becoming More Acquainted with the Four Culprits

When we feel we need to minimize our faults, we may employ some defensive thinking. The trouble is, this thinking keeps us trapped in shame-related behaviors. The four culprits merit a closer look in order to reflect a bit more on the impact of these maneuvers on our relationships and on how we conduct our lives.

Hypocrisy   *Do as I say, not as I do.*

The first and arguably the most common defensive strategy is the use of hypocrisy, Essentially, hypocrisy is finding fault with the behavior of someone else when we are guilty of doing the same thing, If we *have* to be right and fear we might *not* be right, we are compelled to contrive a way to look good (right) to others *and* hide our imperfection. *Not me! I never do that!* Applying the fine art of hypocrisy may give us precious short-term relief from threats to our public image, but by saying one thing and doing another, we drill worm holes in our self-esteem and in our relationships at the same time.

Here's a tip about sniffing out hypocrisy. Whenever there is a discrepancy between the words you hear and the behavior you observe or experience, give more credibility to the behavior. We've all experienced getting a "hit," a knowing that what someone is saying doesn't ring true. Although we don't always confront the confusion or disbelief on the spot, we definitely file it for future reference.

We've come to accept hypocritical declarations as fact. As long as the person delivering the hypocrisy looks good and speaks convincingly, we seem to be conditioned to pay attention to the words being said and not to look at any discrepant *behavior.* A self-declared family-oriented public figure is revealed to have been unfaithful to his partner and denies undeniable documentation of the affair. A clergyperson declares homosexuality to be a sin and secretly engages in a homosexual relationship.

Hypocrisy is widely practiced. There's the case of a father who publicly declares his opposition to abortion, but agrees to pay for his daughter's termination of an untimely pregnancy. In another instance, an adolescent son attempts suicide. His mom, a social worker who does workshops for parents on improving communication with their kids, is called to the emergency room where a bunch of pills is being pumped from her son's stomach. On the way home, after a long silence in the car, the son begins to offer an explanation and the mom quickly says, "I don't want to talk about it."

Being a practitioner of hypocrisy is hard on the soul. It's one way we set ourselves up for a life based on pretending. We feel fake and ungrounded, continually scoping out others for clues as to how we're doing. Perhaps the most distressing discovery is that living hypocritically promotes emotional distance in relationships. A hypocrite is hard to trust because it's hard to tell if they mean what they say. Hypocrisy also keeps distance between ourselves and our integrity.

A forty-something wife, mother, and engineer, had this to say: "I'm angry and sad about having run too many years of my life by 'Don't be who you are' and 'You are not right enough.' The good news is that I'm the one who can change what I learned long ago. Now I do what I believe and I feel more powerful for it."

We must be careful about what we pretend to be.

Kurt Vonnegut

Right/Wrong, Good/Bad, Either/Or, Win/Lose Thinking
My way or the highway.

A hallmark of the Do and Be Right rule is the practice of two-way thinking, one contrary to the other. This device is a way of pinning people down to a forced choice between only two alternatives. If it's not this, it's that. Frequently used by a person wishing to be in control of another's choices, it limits options. *Make up your mind. You either believe in it or you don't.*

Here's how either/or thinking works with young children. The parent of a 2-year-old gives the child choices within narrow limits because 2-year-olds don't have the experience or reasoning to deal with a whole range of options. *Do you want to wear the stripes or the polka dots? Would you like to get in the car under your power or mine?* Two-year-olds are learning they have choices. They need opportunities to experience the outcomes of their choices so they can develop the wisdom, over time, of knowing what's in their best interests. Adults, however, are capable of coping with a wider variety of possibilities.

Believing there's only one way to be *Right* presumes that if I'm not right, I'm wrong. If I'm not good, I must be bad. If it's not this way, then it must be that way. If I'm not with you, I'm against you. If I don't win, I lose. If I'm not *for* something, then I'm against it. But that severely limits solving a problem when there are other possibilities we're blind to considering. Our focus should be on first defining a problem and solving it, not engaging in absolute right-wrong, good-bad battles about who's right.

Such dichotomous thinking can be most evident when speaking about values. Values are beliefs that reflect our ideals, standards, and morals. *You're either a saint or a sinner. I always thought she was a good person. until I learned she was having an affair. All people who belong to that religion are violent. All people who belong to that religion are loving and peaceful.* Must a choice or an error in judgment lock in someone's badness?

An old story illustrates the either/or concept. An impoverished old man desperately needed to get medicine to address his wife's painful condition. The man had a deeply held value against stealing from others. What was he to do? Either allow his wife to suffer or steal the medicine? It is truly a moral dilemma to have to make a choice from those two options, but are there other options to consider? Of course there are. He could appeal to her doctor for samples. He could approach the pharmacist for ideas on how to get the medicine at greatly reduced cost. He could borrow the money. He could ask the pharmacist to work out a manageable payment system. There are almost always more than two options.

To get trapped in good/bad, either/or thinking sets us up to create divisions. It does more to separate and create distance between people than it does to promote better connections. As a matter of fact, using absolute right/wrong thinking prevents honest problem-solving among equals. Imagine being among a group of six seated around a table. In the middle of the table sits a problem to solve. Three on one side reach across the table. The three on the other side respond by shaking the outstretched hands. Both sides hold the handshake, which, in minutes, turns into a grip. The grip gets tighter and tighter and the session becomes a tug-of-war. A stand-off.

Either/or. Win/lose. Then imagine that the problem in the middle of the table is still there.

Imagine the next step in this scenario, one that is repeated time and again in more intimate relationships. *"It's your fault!"* *"If you would only (fill in the blank)."* *"You are unreasonable. What's the use?"*

In intimate relationships, competition to prove who's right or who's at fault can happen over the seemingly unimportant "small stuff" like the toilet seat cover or hair left in the sink. Those "small things" become more about feeling disrespected, unheard, or misunderstood by the partner. And they may be the tip of the iceberg, a clue to something deeper going on.

We shouldn't be surprised that it takes a heap of vulnerability to reveal our inner reality to others. Who doesn't fear being rejected, dismissed, hurt, or even annihilated, if more of who we are becomes known? Feeling that a sort of competition about who was "right" lurked just below the surface, Victor got in touch with how resentful he was. Looking to fix a waning relationship, he approached his wife, Val, about seeing a therapist together.

Victor regretted deferring to his wife's wishes even in cases when he knew he didn't want to. Looking back, Victor said, "I didn't insist on dealing with the problems between us. I couldn't admit I needed help and neither could she. Our relationship just continued to go downhill, and now I can see our kids suffered from the times I didn't stand up to her. It's not all her fault. We both had a big Do Right and Be Right, and we could have saved our marriage if it weren't for the limits of our own emotional vulnerabilities and unwillingness to "give in." Neither of us could tolerate being wrong. Instead, we piled up the defenses and carried on until it made no sense to be together. We hadn't outgrown each other. We'd worn each other out."

If I believe I must be right, and you and I differ in what's right, I dedicate myself to proving you wrong. I will do what is necessary to win this battle, especially when the stakes are high. It won't be pretty and it will drive a wedge between us, but if I *must* win, I will call on authorities or. one way or another. deceive you, humiliate you, or show you contempt. I may even abandon or threaten to abandon you, if not physically, then emotionally. Making the other person fall in line is the goal.

Whenever someone *has* to win, someone *has* to lose. And the tail-between-the-legs feeling of losing is not attractive or desirable. Those who lose have long memories. Resentments build. Observe how win/lose works among friends, couples, organizations, culture groups and nations. There's plenty of room for options not yet considered. *Right* should mean what works that benefits both parties, which means giving up the idea that everything can work perfectly our way.

Instead, with a strong heart, risk being humble, own your part of the dispute, and go for a win-win.

I have not failed. I've just found 10,000 ways that won't work.

Thomas A. Edison

Being Confused and Confusing with Mixed Messages
Come here/go away.

Sometimes we hear two messages about the same thing, one saying one thing and the other saying the opposite. Both messages can make sense individually, but they become confusing when heard and experienced together. It is just flat out impossible to put them together and have one meaning.

I love you/Go away. Be active/Be quiet. I'm glad you were born/You are a bother. Mixed messages don't have to be spoken. One can be spoken and the other message may be a behavior. Consider an "I love you" to a person being battered physically or emotionally. A child must wonder how he should be ashamed and put it together with being told he was made in the likeness and image of God. The "not worthy" message directly opposes the "worthy" one.

- *Shame on you! / You make me proud.*
- *You should know better than that. / You're good at everything!*
- *What's wrong with you? / I can always count on you.*
- *You don't have the brains you were born with. / You are good at figuring things out.*

If a child is more comfortable with the negative messages and suspicious of the positive ones, she just might convert any incoming positives into negatives, thereby unconsciously throwing away her own Good. Sender says: *I love the birthday card you made for me!* Receiver hears: *I should have used better colors. It wasn't very good.*

Mixed messages are a less obvious way that the practitioners of shame rules make us question how we're experiencing reality. In trying to believe what's being said, the recipient of mixed messages is baffled and stuck, not knowing what to believe. The senders of mixed messages, meanwhile, keep from having to be clear about what they mean.

One day, after hearing about mixed messages during a workshop, Mack had a light-dawning breakthrough. The leader said, "Mixed messages are two or more messages that oppose one another. It's not possible to 'come here' and 'go away' at the same time. You can't figure out what to believe, so you stay stuck."

That night, an early memory popped into Mack's mind. He was 6 and sitting on the front porch with his mother and 5-year-old sister Cindy after a summer afternoon rain. The subject of babies came up.

"Where did I come from?" Cindy asked.

"You came out of my tummy," said Mother.

"What about me?" asked Mack.

His mother turned to Mack and said, "You came out of another woman's tummy. You're adopted." Then she quickly added, "But we chose you."

"A mixed message for me," said Mack. "I heard 'You are mine/ you are not mine.' How was I supposed to believe that both were true? I was only 6!"

As an adult, Mack was able to figure out his early confusion. "I know Mom wanted me to think that choosing me was better than the way they got Cindy. What I heard was if someone chooses you, they can also un-choose you. It wasn't a happy thought! She could have just given us the facts and not added the part that implied a comparison of better/worse. That would have been enough for then."

Some hard-core users of the shame rules are masters of mixed messages. Mixed messages keep a sane person confused. As a recipient, if you feel your head is on a rotating swivel, it is. The trouble is, having experienced and internalized mixed messages as best we understood them, we give mixed messages to ourselves. We can keep ourselves confused and stay stuck!

As the poet William Stafford wrote in his poem, A Ritual to Read to Each Other:

"The signals we give . . . yes, no, or maybe

They should be clear, for the darkness around us is deep."

The way to unravel and make sense of mixed messages is to identify what each message means and decide to believe one or the other. It is possible that both are true. That's *ambivalence*. In close relationships, the partners can plumb their depths to understand more about that ambivalence, and move ahead based on what they learn.

We are all looking for a less anxiety-producing, more purposeful, genuine, and love-infused existence. Consider God as another word for Love. God and Love are both okay with mistakes. They're okay with people being learners. We are human and imperfect and worth loving.

And a sense of tomorrow entered their hearts
and never left them again.

Unknown

Being Judgmental   *Don't look here. Look over there.*

Many of us learned and developed superlative judging skills as we grew up. Those around us assured themselves they were right by judging others for being wrong. To be clear, that meant not just judging another's behavior. It meant judging the person for having *engaged* in the behavior.

- *She shouldn't wear that! She has such bad taste in clothes.*
- *What on earth is wrong with him? He's never on time.*
- *Can you believe that Bruce decided to marry her?*
- *His ideas are crazy, crazy, crazy and so is he!*
- *I don't know why she goes to that church!*

Making judgments about someone's wrongness is not the same as making a judgment based on evaluating data. Making that kind of judgment means weighing evidence and making choices, as in "The $20,000 car fits my budget better than the $30,000 one" and "I like the SUV, but the smaller car gets better mileage." This is not the same as judging others as wrong for their choices.

Making judgments based on our opinion of someone else's choices is not useful if we're making the other person bad or wrong so we can feel we're good or better. Their choices and values may not be ours, but that does not make them bad or wrong. In a shame-based system, this kind of judgment is second nature for those who would rather focus on someone else's business than their own.

Being judgmental is a defense mechanism. One effect of making judgments is to keep the spotlight elsewhere rather than paying attention to our own business. By doing so, we avoid addressing our personal pain–of maltreatment, of loss, of injustice, of abandonment, of whatever unfinished business lies waiting in our hearts and souls for our attention.

In an attempt to be engaging, a lecturer speaking about teens in school said, "Better luck next time, Buckwheat!" Later, a member of the audience reported she was offended by the reference to Buckwheat. To her, the lecturer had made fun of Buckwheat, referencing the character in the old Our Gang comedies.

The lecturer explained how Buck was the last name of one of her son's best friends in high school. Her nickname was "Buckwheat" and definitely was meant and received by her as a term of endearment. Buckwheat meant something totally different in the context of someone else's experience.

Both the lecturer and the learner could make judgments of the other and, if left unaddressed, they could miss a chance to understand one another's context and experience.

The lecturer apologized for not knowing about the audience member's sensitivity to the Buckwheat character, although, as she thought about the incident later, she remembered having heard about the negative meaning of the Buckwheat character, but hadn't thought it was important. By discounting the importance of what the character represented to some in the audience, she was disrespecting them too.

Our judgmental selves come out in a flash. Old Rules family members can be so well schooled in making judgments, they become part of the fabric of being alive! Recently, while visiting his daughter's family, Nate found himself blurting out, "Your family should do a better job of recycling." Oops. There it was. What business is it of Nate's how they carry out recycling? Why should it bother him? Answer: Because he believes recycling is right up there next to Godliness. Why wouldn't he want his loved ones to believe and do what is important to him? If Nate needs to comment on recycling practices, he can find a different way to express his wish, and then let go of expectations that his daughter's family should recycle his way.

In making a judgment of another person, what the judger is judging is also likely true of himself. Making judgments of another to make ourselves feel better (more *right*) is really a way to reveal something about our own unrecognized unfinished business. Michelle speaks judgmentally of her friend for grooming her 4-year-old daughter for beauty pageants, while Michelle is busy enrolling her 4-year-old son for any and all sports in season. Steven goes on and on about his friend's poor management of his money, while Steven himself is no sterling example of making good choices about his resources.

We can catch ourselves about to issue a judgment, and stop to ask if we are doing the same thing that we are criticizing others for doing. Author Pema Chodron[10] has written about a most effective way to deal with judgments. First, acknowledge the judgment and change the judgmental words to *wanted or unwanted*. "Being with people who are highly judgmental is unwanted by me. I want to be with people who understand differences and have compassion for those differences." Then, when you encounter a judgment-arousing situation, re-name the judgment as something you don't want for yourself. Breathe the unwanted behavior deeply into yourself, and while it is in your body transform it into what you want instead. Then exhale the unwanted behavior and retain its wanted replacement. On your outbreath, you are letting go of the judgment you have made, not only of others, but of yourself.

Do unto others as you would have them do unto you.

Matthew 7:12

The Process of Disarming the Four Culprits

To intentionally shift from the automatic cooperation with an unwanted ingrained habit, consider beginning with a focus on a single culprit: hypocrisy, either/or, mixed messages, or being judgmental.

First, take the time to observe how that culprit works in the interactions of other people. Watch. Listen. Think. Observe interactions in all settings, in person or on television, the Internet, and elsewhere. After learning what you can from observing how the culprit shows up, become conscious of how you use it in your own life. During this process, resist the urge to be judgmental of yourself. You are engaged in what is essentially a counter-cultural activity, considering that most people play these games to one degree or another. Intervening on your own tendency to judge can feel like swimming against the tide. Last, practice your wanted behavior. If you find yourself playing the either/or game, stop, take a deep breath and shift into your wanted behavior. If you want to catch yourself being hypocritical, making judgments, or giving mixed messages, the process is the same. Identify. Get acquainted with your habit. Employ a new behavior. Practice.

Forgive yourself for not making this shift perfectly. You'll have plenty of time and plenty of opportunities to practice. The goal is not to do it perfectly. It's to do it better.

Angeles Arrien, cultural anthropologist, passed along an ancient truth: What you focus on, expands. Instead of being so focused on the outside stuff we can't control, the wiser part of us knows we're the only ones we can change, so it pays to put our focus there.

_____

When we are misunderstood and judged unfavorably, what good does it do to defend or explain ourselves? It is so much better to say nothing and allow others to judge us as they please.

Therese of Lisieux

_____

NOW WHAT? Replacing the Do and Be Right Rule

The shame system rules are useful in hierarchical situations where unquestioning control by an authority is the rule. In life-threatening situations where there simply isn't time for a committee meeting, an authority's life-saving directions make good sense.

However, if it's an intimate and mutually respectful relationship you want, the Old Rules based on shame cause more misery than benefit, more separation than closeness, more resentment and suspicion than trust.

If you were in a family where the shame rules ruled, try replacing Do and Be Right with a new rule.

**NEW RULE 1: Learn and then learn
again from your mistakes.**

Imagine yourself believing and acting according to this new rule in all your dealings. What difference would it make? First, the New Rule contradicts the old one by allowing for these dynamics in relationships of all kinds:

- Being relieved from the fear and anxiety of being discovered as defective and imperfect
- Having interactions that are respectful of, and responsible to, one another.
- Living in an atmosphere of ease where the parties aren't devoted to taking one another down.
- Having mutuality between parties who feel less defended and more open to intimacy, who experience less fear and more trust.
- Being willing to negotiate differing beliefs in order to strike a balance both can agree to.
- Experiencing a greater feeling of belonging and acceptance.
- Living in a place where there's more room for fun and less room for resentment.
- Experiencing more love.

These are some of the possible, even probable benefits of the New Rule. Decide what works for you without harming either yourself or others. Be respectful and earn the respect of others. Create. Do. Think. Revise. Try again. Above all, see yourself as a *learner.*

Love is when the other person's happiness
is more important than your own.

J. Jackson Brown, Jr.

Imperfect Perfection or Perfect Imperfection

Changing *Do and Be Right* to *Learn and then Learn Again from Your Mistakes* takes consciousness and commitment. Pay attention to the times when you make judgments or compare yourself with others (and always lose), or criticize others and yourself. Pay attention to times when you are automatically using the old ways. Turn your heart and mind to the replacement rule. What would you like to change, to do differently? Practice, not perfection, is what counts.

Jackie had a history of postponing any situation that involved sticking up for what she needed. If she found an error in the cable bill she would put it aside and fret for days, make notes so she was clear about her problem, run what she'd say to the customer service representative over in her mind, and finally, after days of putting herself through misery she would make the call. Even though these calls resulted in her problem being taken care of, she'd go through the same drill the next time.

Jackie had plenty of friends who didn't break a sweat in similar circumstances. "Why do I have such a problem with this?" she asked herself. "Am I missing a skill I'm supposed to have learned? Haven't I quite nicely survived the many times I've agonized over this? Maybe I don't feel entitled to speak up for myself."

Bingo! The entitlement idea struck a chord that led Jackie to see how she expected herself to know and be right about most everything. "I always marveled at my friends who were so clear. They just expected to be heard. No shrillness or intimidation. No pleading."

One day, Jackie worked out a problem with the hardware store clerk and told her friend, "I had a totally different experience today. I caught myself rehearsing my justifications to the clerk when I remembered I could just say, 'I hope you can help me solve this problem' and expect that it would be done. I didn't feel pathetic or apologetic. I remembered that what I needed was worth speaking up for. And it worked! I left the store feeling on top of the world." Later, she would add, "And nobody was mad at me. The clerk was pleasant! I realized I expected an argument and expected to be proven wrong. I know where that came from!"

Posting the Old and New rules side by side is a good reminder of the change you are making. The new rule is waiting for you to make it automatic. Take the time you need. See the Old and New Rule posters in Appendix C.

Remember your first day on a new job. Everything feels awkward. You don't know which parking structure to use. You are baffled by the one-way street system. You find the building but have to ask what floor your department is on. As you sit in your new office, you feel like an alien dropped onto a far planet. You ask a million questions. You tell yourself that all this will become familiar and in two weeks, you won't be spending the effort you are spending on this first day. Someday soon, this will all be installed in your personal operating system.

As some unnamed sage has said, no one likes to be trapped at the closed end of a box canyon. It's hard to stay a victim when you can see the ladder taking you to the ground above.

It is so conceited and timid to be ashamed of one's mistakes. Of course they are mistakes. Go on to the next.

Brenda Ueland

Shame Hooks

A shame hook is much like a PTSD experience. *Ralph drove over a loose manhole cover, and the loud sound pulled him right back to being in a war zone. His brain knew it was a manhole cover but his body had a very different emotional experience. In an instant, he was back on the battlefield. It took him some time and a lot of self-talk to deal with the automatic physical memory connected with the originating trauma.*

The same thing happens around shame experiences. *Anna's autocratic father barked his demands. "Anna! Bring me the hammer!" Scared to ask where it was, she had to figure out where to find it. He grabbed it from her and demanded sarcastically, "What took you so long? I swear you don't have the brains you were born with!"*

As a young adult, Anna now feels like a powerless little mouse whenever she experiences the same 'Can't you ever do it right' message. She might as well be back in the scene with her father.

Our shame hooks exist because they're uniquely connected to our experience and our feelings about that experience. Once Anna learned what was happening, she got the support she needed to stand up respectfully to put-downs. She always wished it had been safe to respond in the hammer incident by saying, "What if *I do* have the brains I was born with?"

Shame hooks are also referred to as *triggers*.

Making the Turn (Shift) to the New Rule

Slipping off the hooks of familiar but outworn behaviors takes practice. A sailor knows that when bringing a boat around to head in the opposite direction, she must pay attention to the wind and currents. Changing course too abruptly swamps the boat. Sailors who do an "about face" know that turning the rudder is only *one* of the adjustments it takes to change directions abruptly. Sailors often get where they want to go by *tacking* or zig-zagging to make use of the wind.

Getting better at noticing when we're on a hook, or when someone or some situation has pushed our buttons, calls for some strategies for slipping the hooks–disengaging from the hot buttons and objectively seeing what's really going on. Here are some ideas for practicing making changes in three areas: noticing, testing ourselves, and practicing.

Noticing

When a memory of past humiliation is triggered, write about the words and behaviors of those around you that triggered that memory and your feelings at the time.

Be alert for times when others are caught in the Do and Be Right rule while resisting the urge to give advice. Do your noticing quietly.

Testing

When you encounter someone who has opinions or beliefs different from yours and they assert that you are wrong, resist the urge to jump into an argument. Ask yourself if you need to prove you're right. Ask questions. Listen to the responses. Keep asking questions. "Do you mean that...?" "Tell me more." "What happens when...?" "Where did you find this information?" Stay calm and centered. Maintain your beliefs and release the other person to have theirs. You don't have to agree just to be agreeable, and you don't *have* to oppose if you disagree. You may want to state your belief to see how the other person reacts. Ask questions. Listen carefully.

Do your best to understand the source of another's beliefs. Bless both of you for having differing opinions while not demeaning or heaping contempt on one another. Compassionate listening and understanding are the underpinnings of respect and loving.

Practicing

Prepare some responses to shaming, saying them surely and thoughtfully when appropriate: "Thanks for your opinion. I'll think about what you said and get back to you" (or not.)

Say "Are you serious?" or "You can't be serious" in a quietly pleasant and puzzled way. This should cast aspersions on the provocateur's comments.

Say "Don't even go there" while slowly shaking your head.

Say with good humor "I don't believe that deserves my attention" and walk away.

Respond calmly with a question asking for more information, following up with more questions that seek even more information. Ask for specifics and clarifications. With sincere interest, keep calmly drilling down.

Cut off the interaction by saying something like "I'll catch up with you later."

Quietly and without telling anyone, for one day, practice believing that your contributions and beliefs are useful in all the day's interactions. You know what you're talking about! Trust your feelings and allow yourself to know what you need. People may have their opinions or advice for you but calmly reassure yourself that you know what you know and don't have to *prove* anything to anyone. Notice what you experience. Practice feeling quietly confident.

Practice restating judgments into statements of what you want and don't want. "I hate people who lie to my face" can be shifted to "I choose to be with people who don't lie to me."

Practice saying "I may not be right" and "I don't know, but I'll find out" or "I'm not sure" of "I may be wrong" as often as necessary to release yourself from being put on the spot.

Here are a couple more thoughts that can help you keep what you want to keep and change what you want to change:

- Groupings of supportive parent messages (affirmations) appear in Appendix B. They are organized rule by rule. Use them to support your turn from the Old Rules to the New. Many of us missed hearing these messages along our way.

- When putting a new rule into practice, consider the value and dynamics of the relationship in question. Having a shame response to a salesperson is a situation we can shrug off. Getting hooked by a person who means a lot to you is different because there's much more vulnerability involved and more risk. Those take both courage to express and a commitment to hang around.

An On-the-spot Way Out of Feeling Ashamed

At those times when you recognize feeling shameful, here's an idea to pull yourself back to knowing what is true. When we're feeling ashamed, the world seems to go flat. It stops. It's like a movie when the film breaks. Like a a flat, two-dimensional picture on a coloring book page. Everything around us stops. Everything around us loses its verve. There's a sudden sense of being outside ourselves and separate from the *you* in the scene you were part of a second before. We are there and not there. This is a shame retreat.

To restore your equilibrium, take a deep breath. Then take another. No matter where you are, in a room or in a forest, tell your eyes to notice the layers of color, the depth of perspective, the rich textures all around you. Ask your eyes to draw out near and far features, making your picture 3-dimensional, replacing the flatness of the 2-dimensional world you see when you're in a shame retreat. Switch the pictures of flatness and wholeness back and forth. You are in charge now. End with the deep, rich, 3-dimensional image. Take another deep breath. Come back to inhabit what is true. Appreciate coming back to yourself. Look around you and marvel at the depth and richness you see there. You are home.[11]

Dealing with Regrets

In making the shift from Old Rules to New Rules, we are inevitably reminded of things we've said and done, or situations we've been in that we regret. If those memories hang around and continue to cause us distress, we can revisit them to find some kind of resolution for ourselves. One reason to clear up a lingering glitch is to feel better about ourselves for having tried.

If you engaged in behavior you regret, ackowleding what you did could involve making an apology. In any case, after taking the responsibility that is yours, it might be time to forgive yourself and let it go.

We've all had those times when we felt publicly ashamed. Edgar does a great motivational speech. He still pulls up short everytime he recalls the time he lost concentration, wandered around his topic, and could hardly wait until it was over. He, the expert, felt like everything he knew had just left the room. By his own evaluation, it was bad. He totally regrets the incident but he's decided not to be terminally bothered by it. He is human, after all.

When we have personal unfinished business with someone, particularly someone important to us, there are other matters at issue. Regretful words and behaviors, unexpressed feelings, a judgment, a put-down. About something either given or received. In either case, these are some tips to remember that help in healing old wounds and wounding.

First, ask the other person if they're willing to have a conversation and then arrange a time and a conducive place to have it.

At the meeting, thank the other person for being willing to meet, for it is your problem you want to clear.

Say *Something's been bothering me* or *I'd like to check something out with you.* Remember to avoid beginning your statements with YOU, which invites immediate defensiveness.

Take the person back to the time of the regretful incident. *Remember when we were playing volleyball at Lake Forest Park last month?*

Be clear about what happened. *After you missed spiking the ball a couple of times, I yelled something like 'Learn how to jump!' I realize I was showing off for the guy next to me, and I've been sad and worried ever since for mouthing off to you. I'd like to think I'm not like that.*

The next step is a heartfelt, *I'm so sorry for what I said.* Then listen and respond. Stay centered in your heart's intention.

When the regret is with someone close to you, the depth of the clearing reflects the relative seriousness of the situation.

One mother failed to protect her 8 year old daughter from a neighborhood boy who was six years older. The daughter asked for permission to go to the boy's house to see his new camera. Mom said no. Dad said it was okay. Mom backed down.

Years after this incident, during a therapy session the daughter told her mom what had happened. Mom heard the whole story, cried with her daughter, and then said, "I am so sorry I put preserving my relationship over acting on what you needed. I should have protected you. I wish I had known better and done better. I love you with all my heart, I regret letting you down more than you'll ever know."

We must listen to the response and follow through with the conversation that ensues. Put aside the tendency to defend your actions. Hear the impact your behavior had on someone else, difficult though it may be. Stand in the calm of believing the other person may need to discharge their feelings.

You can ask what you can do to make amends when the conversation seems to be nearing an end. There might be an amends you have in mind. If so, ask if the other person is willing to accept it. Making amends is a way to re-build broken bridges. In either case, indicate your intention to avoid such disregard for either your or the other person's needs in the future. Invite further feedback if you want it. We are learners, after all.

How does dealing with regrets relate to the Do and Be Right rule? Most everyone has fallen victim to believing and living by the rule. Most everyone has cooperated with the rule and left unfinished business dangling in their memories. Repairing the ones we can repair is part of addressing some gnawing shame leftovers so we aren't, even unconsciously, dragging them around. Forgiving ourselves for making mistakes around things we didn't know how to do differently is also part of clearing our field in order to move ahead.

A bird does not sing because it has an answer.
It sings because it has a song.

Chinese proverb

Moving On

Putting out a persona of perfection is like being in a swimming pool and trying to keep five soccer balls underwater at the same time. It's impossible. It's tiring. It's hard on the soul to live in fear of tripping up and being exposed as counterfeit. Using the replacement rule encourages acting in ways more congruent with the beings we are meant to be. And it blows soft air to fan our individual lights to brightness.

Next, we'll take a look at one of the most pervasive characteristics of a shame environment: re-directing the attention of those who might see our so-called imperfections.

Ritual to Read to Each Other
By William Stafford

If you don't know the kind of person I am
and I don't know the kind of person you are
a pattern that others made may prevail in the world
and following the wrong god home we may miss our star.

For there is many a small betrayal in the mind,
a shrug that lets the fragile sequence break
sending with shouts the horrible errors of childhood
storming out to play through the broken dyke.

And as elephants parade holding each elephant's tail,
but if one wanders the circus won't find the park,
I call it cruel and maybe the root of all cruelty
to know what occurs but not recognize the fact.

And so I appeal to a voice, to something shadowy,
a remote important region in all who talk:
though we could fool each other, we should consider—
lest the parade of our mutual life get lost in the dark.

For it is important that awake people be awake,
or a breaking line may discourage them back to sleep;
the signals we give—yes or no, or maybe—
should be clear: the darkness around us is deep.

CHAPTER FIVE

OLD RULE 2: BLAME

**When you make a mistake or get blamed for
something, pass the blame elsewhere.**

*When Jack, now 50, recently had dinner with his older sister,
he stared at the candles she lit and started to chuckle. "Remember
the time when we were kids, and we got home from a week at the
lake? It had been so hot...."*

*"Oh, I still think about that!" Lauren almost blew out the
candle with her laughter. "I remember yelling at everyone, 'Look!
Look at the candles!' They were really tall, but they had bent over
double from the heat."*

*Jack gestured with his fork. "Yes! And then you said we should
light them to see if the flame went up or down." Their laughter
re-erupted.*

*Lauren wiped her eyes with her napkin. "I must have been
about 10 then. Mom gave me her best 'You've got to be kidding'
look. I was, as you know, the Good Girl."*

*Jack's smile faded. "But then she saw the candles the next day
and asked you if you had done it."*

"Remember her stern look?" Lauren narrowed her eyes and cleared her throat to sound like their mother. 'Who lit my candles?'

"You gave her your ' Who me?' look of innocence and said, 'It wasn't me! It must have been Jack!' When Mom turned to me, I told her I didn't do it....'"

Lauren set her spoon down. "Sorry about that. At least she didn't punish you."

Jack touched the trickle of wax dripping down the candle. "No, you got by with it, but I still regret that she thought I was a liar."

WHAT? The Meaning of the Old Blame Rule

Blaming: A Clue to Irresponsibility

"It's all his fault!" or "I didn't have anything to do with it."

Blaming others for something we've done or not done is a mechanism of self-protection. When the roving spotlight of Do and Be Right zeroes in on us, we want to get rid of the fearful exposure of our perceived weakness or failure as fast as we can. We do *not* want to be seen as wrong or flawed. If we can successfully divert the spotlight, chances are good that our perceived inadequacies will escape scrutiny. If we succeed, we're relieved.

So we blame another person, process or thing. My friend, the time of day, the boss, the road crew, grass that grows too fast...absolutely anything is fair game, even it if makes no sense. Unfurled, the banner that the blamer carries declares, "It's not my fault!"

Consider the example of a coach who angrily yells at a player for making mistakes. Might the coach be blaming the player to avoid his responsibility to tell the player how to improve her performance? "You've missed every 3-pointer you've shot" instead of "Get your body in this position (coach demonstrates) before you launch the ball."

To find a fault is easy; to do better may be difficult.

Plutarch

How to Tell if You Are the Target

Have you ever felt as though you've unexpectedly had a fist thrust into your midsection? Whomp! Have you experienced a feeling in the pit of your stomach that meant "What was that?" or had a startling, if quiet, moment that left you asking yourself, "What in the world is going on?" or "What did I do wrong?" or "What just happened?" Lucy remembers just such a moment.

Lucy developed and hosted a two-day seminar. Participants seemed involved and engaged, and their evaluations gave high ratings for positive content and relevance to both their jobs and personal lives. The next week a colleague stopped Lucy to say how sorry she was about the workshop. "I heard it really bombed—that people were so disappointed, many left early."

Lucy was so surprised she didn't know how to respond. She did remember one person leaving early to attend a funeral. She checked with the workshop's sponsors. Not only were they happy with the evaluations, but several of the agency's staff had attended most of the seminar.

All became clear when Lucy found out that the rumor was

started by a woman who had wanted the job of developing the workshop. She had been passed over in favor of Lucy. "I learned a lot from this," said Lucy. "If that kind of hit happens again, I'll decide whether to confront the person or just let it go. From now on, I'll remember to check my reality, and if there is something I did or said that I wish I could do over, I can own up to my part. I realize this is a great improvement because too many times I've jumped to thinking if something bad happened it was all my fault."

Startle and momentary disbelief are a body's reaction to something being horribly out of place, out of sync. That's a clue that we may be being blamed. When we're shocked by what feels like an out-of-the-blue attack, we feel threatened and we're totally unaware of the reason. Our defensive shield goes up. "What did I do? What you are asserting or claiming about me does not compute with my reality. Am I crazy?" And we might jump right in by blaming back!

When someone's claim about you makes no factual or reasonable sense, you may be being blamed for whatever serves the blamer's needs. The bigger the discrepancy between the blamer's assertions and the reality of the person being blamed, the bigger the problem. In any case, the *blamee* is likely to be filled with extreme uncertainty and confusion.

Might the blame being cast on someone else also be true of the one doing the blaming? The one who blames is almost always unconsciously talking about their own irresponsibility or issues.

In any case, the Blame Game is an endless merry-go-round of irresponsibility. John blames George. George defends by turning the blame back onto John–or onto something or someone else, Round and round it goes. At the end, the original question or problem goes unanswered and unsolved. Responsibility drops into the abyss.

To stop the merry-go-round, the participants can lay claim to their individual responsibility for the situation. It's a celebration when all parties agree to do this! Wrinkles get ironed out. Respect for one another deepens. However, when one or the other chooses not to own their part, it's easy to suspect that an unaddressed and lurking need or problem is standing in the way of an improved relationship. Solving a problem and improving a relationship are not going to happen when blaming remains present.

As the person blamed, the challenge is always to decide if we'll own our part, let it go, or engage in a fight to the finish with the blamer. Mutual take-downs to win the Who's Right? question result in more trouble, not less. In a shame-based system there's a target on everyone's back.

Take your life in your own hands, and what happens?
A terrible thing: no one to blame.

Erica Jong

SO WHAT? Some Effects of the Blame Rule

What Difference Does it Make?

Interestingly enough, blaming others doesn't get the blamer off the hook. There is an unintended consequence to the blamer of blaming to avoid responsibility.

73

A student knocked on my office door the day after attending a class I taught on the dynamics of adoption. After a few warm-up exchanges, she told me she was a birth mother who relinquished her son to adoptive parents. For the ensuing years, she blamed her parents for forcing her to "give up" her child.

I listened to her story and it was clear I needed to support her in talking about her lingering pain with her therapist. A month later, the student knocked on my door again. She seemed softer, more relaxed.

"I 'got it' about the relinquishment of my son," she said. "I had always blamed my parents for making me sign those papers. They had made it clear they were not willing to help me raise my baby and if I decided to parent him, their support would not include bringing the baby home to their house. I was in college and I wanted to get my degree. All these years, I held a resentment and blamed them, but I was the one who signed the papers. I didn't want to give up the baby, but I also couldn't see myself as a student struggling to raise a child on my own."

"Here's the thing," she continued. "Since I took responsibility for making that decision and for signing the papers, I have felt a degree of power I have seldom felt before. And the unexpected surprise? I have felt an increased sense of personal power in all areas of my life now. I like it! And I'm not hiding anymore."

And so it is. Accepting responsibility results in feeling a heightened sense of personal power, while blaming chips away at one's integrity.

The Tools of the Blamer Trade

In order to become more conscious of a possible vulnerability to being blamed, start a list of blamer strategies like the one below. Feel free to edit or expand it according to your experience. Remember the blamer's goal: to avoid responsibility and distract from the truth. To that end, a blamer may:

- Accuse the blamee. *It's all your fault.*
- Begin the first sentence with "You" when talking to the blamee.
- Call the blamee names. *Liar!*
- Make judgments and negative inferences about the blamee's character or behavior.
- Cite a list of historical infractions by the blamee.
- Criticize with all-inclusive words like *You never...you always...*
- Sarcastically minimize the problem or its impact. *It's no big deal.*
- Show looks of contempt, disinterest, or disregard.
- Shrug shoulders to send a *who cares?* message.

If we recognize when we're getting blamed, we can figure out what's happening and avoid getting hooked into believing it's either not our fault at all or is *entirely* our fault. Conversely, if we hear ourselves blaming others, it's time to take a break and give some thought to the situation and our part in it.

Blaming is a first-line tool for someone whose unconscious goal is to get another person to over-function on their behalf. *You don't pay enough attention to me.* Well, there's a fine hook! If we bite, we set about working hard to give the person whatever we think constitutes enough attention.

There is a better way. If the first person asks the second person for time to do something enjoyable or just to hang out together, the ground is laid to work out a plan or have a longer conversation, both of which presumably satisfies the need for attention.

A *You don't pay enough attention to me* can initiate a round of mutual blaming. However, for some of us, it means an invitation for the blamee to try harder. But by over-functioning on someone else's behalf, I may be under-functioning for myself. Another way to say that is by being over-responsible for others, I am being under-responsible to myself. Blaming is a giant-sized hook.

That's how it goes for adults, but what if you're a child? When a child is blamed, they're likely to believe it. *You make me nervous. You'll be the death of me. No wonder I'm so grumpy!* Worse yet, if they experience all manner of abuse, they are blamed for something they may not have the power or means to do anything about. In their developing and egocentric minds, they think they are the ones at fault because, after all, the grown-ups represent all they know about authority. As such, *the adult* must be right. This form of blame tends to stick around and gets woven into their pictures of who they perceive themselves to be.

A man can get discouraged many times but he is not a failure until he begins to blame somebody else and stops trying.

John Burroughs

Several Common Blame Situations

As you observe blaming in action, two scenarios often show up: blaming to stop or impede another's progress, and mutual blaming that makes certain whatever mischief is going on will keep going on.

There are black belt players of the Blame Game who use the scurrilous tactic of false public attacks in order to shut down an adversary. How does one respond to a blame attack willingly shared with anyone who will listen? Deny the accusation? *No, that's not true.* Once the blamer has the platform, they issue another statement that throws fuel on the flames of the first. The usual response: *No, that is **absolutely not true**! Her assertion is **totally false**!* Paradoxically, the harder the blamee denies the accusation, the guiltier they look.

The first arrow of a public blaming has a way of sticking, even though the accusation (blame) is false. Those whose goal is to take down another person know this well. It helps them avoid talking about whatever they'd rather avoid. It distracts from the real issue by keeping the spotlight off the blamer.

The second common blame situation is one that is familiar to most people in close relationships. It is the Blame Stand-off, a deeper level of merry-go-rounding. Here's how it works. Judy blames George for the problem. George blames Judy for the problem. George then blames Judy for the *last* problem. Judy blames George for that problem and the one before that. And so on. They blame one another into an ugly place and still haven't solved the problem. They just postpone it by kicking it down the road. But it never really goes away. It just hangs around and festers. Neither of them is happy or feeling more trusting of one another because they have avoided the real conflict between them. If they only knew. They have missed a chance to be closer and feel better about themselves and one another by taking the responsibility that belongs to them.

> *Your true mate is not a person to be encountered*
> *but a new depth to be discovered in yourself.*
>
> Eric Butterworth

Conflict happens. We're not carbon copies of one another, all wanting the same thing, having the same needs and beliefs, sharing every idiosyncrasy. Many of us lack the skills to get us through conflict to connection. Most of us are not all that practiced in resolving conflict. Nor do we have an abundance of role models. If there were ever a time to get some third-party help to learn the skills of resolving conflict, this is it.[12]

> *Let everyone sweep in front of his own door,*
> *and the whole world will be clean.*
>
> Goethe

Everyday Blaming (excuses)

One morning I left my office hurriedly and made my way to an interview where a group was to decide if they were going to hire me for a consulting job. After ten minutes on the road, I realized I was in big trouble. I glanced at the clock, hoping I had misread the numbers. No, the numbers wouldn't move. I was going to be really late. I began rehearsing my apology. I had encountered road construction, traffic, and maybe even some other impeding disaster–if I could come up with a plausible one. I stopped short. What was I doing?

I arrived 20 minutes late and this was what I said: "I apologize. I'm so sorry I am late. I made the mistake of taking a last minute phone call before I left the office and I honestly had not allowed enough time to get here, especially since I'd never been here before." Whew! My apology was accepted. They assured me they spent the time until my arrival getting something else accomplished. Whew again!

I accepted responsibility for my behavior. I felt centered and clear during our meeting. I can't help but wonder how I might have felt about myself and how the meeting might have gone differently if I had begun by blaming circumstances rather than stating the truth.

Blame in Rumor's Clothing

Most of us have experienced being the target of gossip and wonder what we can do about it. Harry Illsley was a respected community leader and organizer of a farmers' cooperative in the 1930s. He taught his children a set of clear, simple, and elegant options for when one is on the receiving end of a rumor. They could choose which way or ways would work for them, depending on the situation.

- Address the rumor immediately.
- Refrain from honoring the rumor by responding to it.
- Wait and see.

In any case, some thinking time to decide which choice fits the situation is a good idea. Re-construct the situation in your mind. Talk with others you trust to be straight with you. Ask yourself how you might have unintentionally contributed to the situation. Clean up what there is to clean up. Stand in your truth. Especially, be true to yourself. You should not have to experience distress every time someone floats a rumor about you. Nor should others get away with spreading rumors by contaminating your life to get what *they* need.

NOW WHAT? Replacing the Blame Rule

**NEW RULE 2: Accept responsibility
for your decisions and behaviors.**

Responsibility Instead of Blame

As a fledgling student teacher for a sixth grade class, I soon learned that part of my job was to make a final call in disputes. When students were lined up for lunch or recess, every so often, an obvious difference of opinion would break out, evidenced by pushing and shoving–or something worse. As I would approach these disruptions to see what was happening, I'd meet a sea of pointing fingers with accusatory words to match. *He pushed me. She looked at me. I did not. He called me a dork!* Unraveling competing blames got old really fast. Frustrated by my insecurity about being fair to the parties, I developed a "I want you to know what I know" speech, which I delivered on the first day of school, with deep sincerity and good humor, as follows:

Here's what I know about how the human body works. Bones don't move by themselves. When arms, legs, and mouths move, muscles do the moving of the bones to which they're attached. Further, muscles don't move unless they receive a signal from nerves. Nerves are the means by which the brain communicates with the muscles. Some of the signals the brain sends work automatically, like keeping your heart going. Other signals the brain sends are a direct result of a decision in the brain to send them, like when you want to pick up a pencil. The brain says "Pick up the pencil" and the hand picks up the pencil.

Therefore, please know what I know. If your arm hits someone, your body merely responded to your brain's decision to hit. So here's how it is. On those rare occasions when I am compelled to respond to an argument or fight, I listen only to the people actually involved. You may report your part only. I will not be listening to any blaming. Period.

Funny how quickly the students learned there was no benefit in escalating trouble in hopes of dumping their poor judgment on someone else. If the disputing parties did not accept their individual responsibilities, it became *my* job to adjudicate the dispute and I assured them, should that be the case, no one would wind up happy! They'd silently be doing some cleaning in the classroom to give them time to think, after which I was happy to hear a story beginning with the word "I."

Being Blamed

In a situation where you're blind-sided, stop and ask yourself what just happened. Resist any urges to strike back or engage in a one-for-one blame-trading festival.

1. Pause to recover. Then respond with either:
   a. A statement like *I'll think about what you said and get back to you.*
   b. A request for clarification. Ask a question about the "situation of concern." Keep asking for clarification until you get it. *Do you mean that...?* After several attempts and if you're not getting clarification, say *I still don't understand"* and leave the encounter.
2. How much responsibility properly belongs to me? How much belongs to the other person?
3. Accept responsibility for your part.
4. If an apology is appropriate, apologize. Otherwise, leave the ball in the other person's court.
5. Do not accept blame that isn't yours.
6. You may want to check your history to understand more about the origin of what hooked you. Is this current situation an echo of a past one?
7. When it's not safe to engage in this kind of interaction, get help to connect or get out.

Learning from Life

Experiencing the consequences of our choices can be life's greatest teacher. Protecting young children over age 3 from the consequences of their choices, unless the threat of physical damage is involved, amounts to preventing them from learning how to manage themselves and their lives. And it's disrespectful to the child.

A first-time mom of a 16-month old warned him not to go out the open front door. When he took a step outside, Mom said, "Come back here!" He did not comply and took another step. Mom rose quickly from her chair, grabbed him, swatted him on the backside and said gruffly, "You listen to what I tell you!"

Knowing about children's development could have prevented blaming and punishing the child for being 16 months old and having a 16-month-old's brain. Before the age of 18 months or so, adults are still responsible for thinking for the child. Either close the door, put up a gate, or bring the child indoors and direct his attention elsewhere. The child in this case was punished for something that was not a matter of his fault or responsibility.

The tendency to use blaming as a way to avoid responsibility has several unwanted ramifications. Whether the blame is implicit or explicit, children who feel blamed are generally less motivated to try again for fear of further failure. Blaming reduces children's confidence. No parent or mentor wishes to lessen the confidence of a youngster they care so much about.

A man who immigrated to the United States from Kenya[13] as an adult describes the way children were mentored when he was growing up.

The core of the method involved first letting natural consequences do the teaching, and second, using the patience of the mentor. First, the child learned by watching and listening to mentoring adults as they solved life's daily situations. Whenever the child's choices had an unsatisfactory or hurtful outcome, adults regarded the child thoughtfully, without criticism or blame. They believed in the child's ability to think. They expected the child to learn from what had worked well and what hadn't. They expected the child to try again. The child knew by looking at the quiet pleasure on the adult faces whether or not they succeeded. Pride in one's accomplishments is a good thing.

Mostly, the adult listened and asked questions to stir the child's thinking, but not in the way an adult's questions are often geared to lead the child to do something the adult's way. It's as if the adults were saying "You can figure out what will work better. Go for a better outcome!" If guidance were needed, it was given calmly and without blame or frustration or criticism of the learner.

Sadly, according to this gentleman's story, as the people supplanted some of their traditional ways, blame and fault-finding began to be more widely used as teaching tools.

Coming Out of Shame

Accepting responsibility can be scary. When we transition from words and behaviors anchored in shame, it's awkward. It can also feel dangerous to come from an unfamiliar place when we're not sure how it will work out. For instance, no matter how dedicated Taylor was to doing what she thought was right, her mother found something wrong. One term Taylor brought home five A's and a B on her report card. Her mother said nothing about the five A's and asked only what the B grade was about. As an adult, Taylor hesitated to advance her ideas and opinions because she was afraid others would find something wrong with them. She felt safer piggy-backing on someone else's. At 45, Taylor is beginning to risk putting her ideas forward and learning to handle her fear of being exposed as wrong. She reported, "I notice I've stopped worrying if my idea will be the best one. Now I put something on the table and know that, in some way, it belongs there and it doesn't have to be better than everyone else's. I'm still a little disappointed my idea wasn't approved as *best,* but oh, well. I'm present and in the game."

Accepting responsibility for our choices is the bedrock of being seen as reliable and trustworthy.

Piglet sidled up to Pooh from behind. "Pooh?" he whispered.
"Yes, Piglet?"
"Nothing," said Piglet, taking Pooh's hand.
"I just wanted to be sure of you."

A.A. Milne

Slipping the Hooks, Making the Turn

So how do we carry a new awareness about blaming into all our relationships? We don't have to revolutionize our behaviors overnight. Unless we're already convinced of the immediate harm blaming causes, it's helpful to first observe blaming at work, in ourselves and in others. Take your time. Implementing any replacement rule needs a full buy-in. Jumping in too fast can result in feeling overwhelmed too soon. Here's a place to begin.

- Make a list of times when you know you have been irresponsible and identify what you might have done instead. Being scrupulously honest with ourselves is for those who are willing to be imperfect. In a real sense, coming clean means coming to terms with our choices–or failures. Overcoming the fear of not being and doing right involves first getting right with ourselves. This is necessary if we are to come out from under the rock where we may have been hiding.

- Raise your consciousness. When you feel blamed, take responsibility when it is yours to take. Leave others' responsibility to them. Acknowledge how you feel when you accept responsibility and when you duck it, if you do. **Resist the urge to judge yourself.**

- Carry a new message in your head: *When I am blamed, I will take the time I need to decide how to respond. I don't have to hurry. I can take my time.* Trust your mind, heart, intuition, and body senses to know when you are being blamed. Take at least three deep breaths or take a time-out to give some thought to what's happening. Take two days if you need to. Or longer. If part of what you are being blamed for is yours, accept responsibility for only that part. The rest goes back to the blamer, where it belongs.

- Practice interfering with any tendency to use the word *you* when you mean *I*. Beginning an interaction with a blaming statement rarely works to our advantage. *You weren't there on time. You didn't feed the dog.* It's a safe bet that the receiver's defenses will be sky high at a time when our goal is to be heard, as in the following:

You were late for school today.   You didn't wake me up on time.

You failed the test?	You didn't make me study for it.
You don't care how I feel!	Look who's talking!

- When *you* statements find their way out and you see the intended receiver stiffen, apologize. Try counting to 10 and saying what you mean in a different, and hopefully, more easily received way.

- Observe your own tendency to blame and ask why accepting responsibility is more difficult in some areas or situations than in others. Try to identify those areas where you respond automatically with blaming. This may help you to know where old habits are still in charge. Remember that blaming was something you learned to do as a child in order to protect yourself in situations that felt life-threatening, or at least, security-threatening.

- **Particularly for parents:** Read and reflect on Russ's story: *Russ had a tendency to blame himself, which both his mom and dad recognized as positive and negative for their son. He accepted responsibility for his decisions, but simultaneously reverted too quickly to blaming himself. "What's wrong with me?" Russ's parents saw a certain resolved sense of personal failure they'd seen a lot. They knew they needed to confront Russ's tendency to beat himself up, so they'd answer his question with "Absolutely nothing," followed by "Did you make a mistake?" and "Can you fix it? What would you do next time?"*

87

It takes attention and courage to get a boat's rudder moved enough to steer a new course, but the boat tips over if the rudder is too abruptly applied! Change always involves some level of risk because it involves using an unfamiliar or untested behavior. "Risk" means not being able to predict exactly what will happen ahead of time. There are always unfamiliar sandbars and a few deadheads just below the water's surface. But with mindfulness and persistence, you can get your boat going where you'd like it to go.

- Reflect on the affirmations in Appendix B for recovering from automatic blaming.
- Celebrate wildly all the ways you already accept responsibility for your thoughts, feelings, and actions!

You are not responsible for the programming
you picked up in childhood.
However, as an adult, you are one hundred
percent responsible for fixing it.

Ken Keyes, Jr.

And the Biggest Benefit Is...

Nothing beats the feeling of standing up to accept responsibility, especially because it's one of the things that builds a track record of integrity. Mean what we say; say what we mean. Interestingly enough, the feeling of *rectitude*, having a sense of moral strength, is worth its weight in gold, for no one can take that away. It's all ours. David's story is about feeling that sense of rectitude by doing the moral thing.

In fourth grade, David found a $20 bill on the playground. He swooped it up and headed for the principal's office. Bystanders couldn't believe it. "What are you doing, man? Finders keepers, losers weepers. That money is yours!"

David hesitated for half a second and continued on his way. He was well thanked by the surprised school secretary. He returned to the playground only to have some of the kids continue to hassle him. The next day, a first grade teacher sought him out. "Thank you for returning my money," she said. "It fell out of my pocket at recess. I never expected to see it again." David later admitted to being a little disappointed that the teacher hadn't given him a small reward!

David could have blamed the teacher for losing the money, soothing his conscience if he were to have kept it. But he didn't. He's an adult now and still smiles when his family tells the story.

People are unreasonable, illogical, and self-centered.
Love them anyway.

Mother Theresa

Moving On

Whenever we hear someone blaming, we can be reasonably certain there's a problem that isn't being solved or something about ourselves we're afraid doesn't pass muster, or wanting to keep our mistakes a secret.

If we fully comply with the next rule, we're shutting down probably the best and most reliable tool helping us discover more about ourselves. Feelings are often trivialized, but they're anything but trivial.

Going in Circles
by Thich Nhat Hanh

O you who are going in circles,
please stop.
What are you doing it for?

> "I cannot be without going
> because I don't know where to go.
> That's why I go in circles."

O you who are going in circles,
please stop.

> "But if I stop going,
> I will stop being."

O my friend who is going in circles,
you are not one with
this crazy business of going in circles.
You may enjoy going,
but not going in circles.

> "Where can I go?"

Go where you can find your beloved
Where you can find yourself.

Thich Nhat Hanh. "Going in Circles" from *Call Me By My True Names: The Collected Poems of Thich Nhat Hanh.* Permission to reprint granted by Parallax Press, Berkeley, CA.

CHAPTER SIX

OLD RULE 3: IGNORE FEELINGS

***Do not acknowledge your feelings
about what's going on.***

Grace was surprised to learn how many people are scared of their feelings. She'd thought she was the only one! Her first therapist said, "You appear to be angry." Her quick reply was "No, I'm not!" Grace thought the therapist's comment was accusatory, implying there was something wrong with her.

The experience reverberated in Grace's mind. She asked herself, "What does she know that I don't? Why was I especially defensive about anger?" As she came into more awareness bit by bit, Grace came to have more compassion for herself and more awareness that she was, indeed, angry. "As I grew up, my parents didn't know how to handle my feelings or help me with them. I heard things like 'If you're going to be mad, Missy, go to your room.' No wonder I learned to deny I had them. The trouble is, pushing my anger down also pushed down my joy."

WHAT? The Meaning of the Old Ignore Feelings Rule

Learning about Feelings

What was so bad about feelings? The answer for Grace lay in remembering what she'd learned in her family.

Grace's grandfather was rigid, controlling, and harshly authoritarian. He selected the careers for his five children and the careers he selected were based on what he needed: business and accounting for two sons to help him manage his large general store; nurse's training for a daughter who would care for his aged mother; and advanced piano instruction for my mother, so she could play for church. The youngest son, the black sheep, was enrolled in college and headed for a business career until he bolted after his freshman year. He was the object of other family members' raised eyebrows. They shook their heads while sharing yet another "tsk,tsk, tsk" story of his so-called exploits.

Grace's mother was afraid of her father's response to every decision and choice she made. For instance, when her mother used the second-hand vacuum cleaner her Dad bought, he stood posted at the window to make sure Grandpa, who lived next door, wouldn't hear it. Mother said he'd have taken them to the woodshed for spending money when a broom would do just as well.

Grace remembered her grandmother as kind and caring. She also remembered her tiptoeing around Grandpa and being especially skilled at protecting herself and her children from his controlling anger.

"My mother passed along some of her experiences with her father in her messages to me. 'Stop those tears or I'll give you

something to cry about! Now get to your room!' 'Don't be mad at your brother. You look ugly when you're mad' and more.

Grace's dad was orphaned at age 3. He was raised by relatives and only occasionally visited by his father. Grace didn't recall any stories about his growing-up years, except that he worked hard helping his grandparents on the farm. "Dad's adolescence was spent during the Depression, when people did what they had to do. No time for feelings! Mother said she agreed to marry Dad partly because she felt sorry for him."

That was the tip of the iceberg in terms of uncovering all the messages about feelings Grace took in from others and played over and over to herself. She says she decided:

- My feelings don't matter.
- My feelings are ignored, minimized, ridiculed, or punished if others even recognize they exist.
- Better to swallow feelings, or put them aside, and get on with my business.
- If I have feelings, hide them from others. If I have them, I'll have them in private.

As she looked back at how she learned to regard feelings, she realized she thought that being angry meant there was something wrong with her! And because her anger wasn't received well by her parents, it isn't hard to figure out why she was so good at stuffing it. No one ever told her that being angry was simply a signal there was a problem to solve.

When Grace learned that feeling angry was telling her that she'd been hurt by being discounted, or having to go without what she needed, or had otherwise been taken advantage of, it wasn't so hard to begin thinking about her anger positively. Anger was just information about something that needed her attention!

Grace didn't blame her family because they hadn't learned it in their families either, so how could they teach or model anything different for her? But she was grateful for seeing her feelings weren't bad. They were necessary.

Eyes that do not cry, do not see.

Swedish Proverb

SO WHAT? Some Effects of the Ignore Feelings Rule

You Can't Be Serious

The Old Rule about ignoring feelings is often interpreted as meaning *don't have feelings*, which is impossible. We can't *not* have feelings. When we are born, we are born with the capacity to feel. We were given this capacity to help us stay alive. Feelings are meant to help us survive by giving us information about our circumstances.

But feelings tell the truth. They will be disregarded, or even punished, in a family not prepared to deal with the truth. Some of us, wisely and for our own good, push our "dangerous" feelings into a deep place for short-term safety and sanity. Over time, this short-term denial of feelings expands to long-term separation from our feelings, a condition dangerous to our well-being. All too soon, we come to discount our own feelings, just as they were regularly discounted by our significant others.

I think of feelings like the black box that keeps a record of an airplane's flight data. The Feelings Black Box serves the same purpose for us. It keeps the data of significance about our personal journeys.

Love never dies a natural death. It dies because we don't know how to replenish its source. It dies of blindness and errors and betrayals. It dies of illness and wounds. It dies of weariness, of witherings, of tarnishings.

Anais Nin

Four Basic Emotions

As we begin to look at our feelings life, let's start with four of the most basic emotions: glad, sad, mad, scared. Happiness tells us we're safe and gives us a sense of wholeness. Sadness signals change, and most often, loss. Anger tells us we're being discounted. Scared or afraid signals we're not safe.

Glad This is what I call the "all's right with the world" feeling. A friend calls it a "tail-wagging" moment. When Jo's son Nathan was separated from his fellow climbers during a storm on Mt. Everest, she said, "I felt like my arm had been cut off." Upon hearing about his rescue, she cried and jumped up and down. "I thought about throwing a big party, but Nathan only wanted to come home and pop popcorn in the fireplace like we did when he was a kid."

Sad Sadness is about losses, big and small. It's a signal we've lost something important to us or something in our environment has changed. There's the sadness that passes quickly when a favorite team loses a game. But when we lose people who have a big place in our lives, we pass through sadness slowly because of their importance to us.

Molly's family moved five times when she was in elementary school. Each time she was sad and each time she was simply told, "You'll make friends in the new town." When her parents divorced, both told Molly they loved her and that they'd always be a family but just would not be living together. Molly sobbed softly in her room. She knew things would never be the same.

Acknowledging feelings of sadness tells us to "gentle up" and give ourselves permission to take the time to engage in what we find nourishing. To "get over it and move on" constitutes a dangerous denial of the very human and humane process of letting go and adjusting to change.

Mad Think of the last time you had reason to feel angry or, at the very least, resentful. Ask yourself this: Were you being put down, ignored, criticized harshly or unjustly? Did someone take something from you without your permission? Did you give something to someone without really wanting to give? You can be grateful for your anger because it signals that it's time to name the problem that needs attention. Paying attention to feelings of anger is a terrific idea, much better than several unattractive (and unproductive) ways of acting them out!

Mark and Ann noticed themselves getting mad when their children expected more and contributed less—with an attitude. Mark announced, "From now on, when either of us begins to resent you, our services and your privileges are suspended until Mom and I conference to decide what's going on and what to do about it." They learned that acknowledging their resentment without ramping up their anger, was good for them, and, coincidentally, good for their children.

Scared Feeling scared is extremely helpful if our goal is staying alive. If a tiger comes into the house, my fear tells me my life may be in jeopardy. I should get myself to a safer place. If I don't feel afraid, I might stand there and be eaten!

A dad who was taking pictures of a bear in Yellowstone thought he was at a safe distance until his children screamed, "Dad, move!" The bear looked far enough away in the viewfinder but was actually much closer. Dad moved away with quick dispatch and was hailed as a quick responder by a relieved family.

There are multiple nuances in the realm of feelings. Being aware of the information they provide works well if you want your life to be real. Real lives are up and down, ebb and flow, gain and loss, joy and sorrow. People with real lives pay good attention to what's going on and what they need.

You can close your eyes to the things you do not want to see, but you cannot close your heart to the things you do not want to feel.

Unknown

Dumbing Down, Numbing Out

Developing a numbness to feelings can be a safety device in a family that disregards or punishes children who express them. Why? Because feelings tell the truth. A family living by the old shame rules can't stand the truth because it disturbs the way the family is functioning. Over time they've arrived at a silent agreement about what's okay and what's not okay. *Don't say anything to Ginger that will set her off. Why does Mom come home from the office so late? Dad, why aren't you talking to Mom?* To acknowledge your true feelings calls attention to something that will disturb the status quo. A *You shouldn't feel that way* response can attempt to derail the question. A *Never mind!* or something harsher, ups the ante. The family has a big stake in shutting the truth-teller down because they unmindfully want to avoid any possibility of being exposed for anything going wrong. Besides, the truth might threaten the balance and façade of the family.

Six-year-old Henry runs to his mom after his dad throws an empty beer can at him. "Daddy scared me."

"Don't be scared." Smiling, his mom ruffles his hair. "Go out and play."

Worse than having feelings disregarded is having it become dangerous to express them. *Henry picks up the beer can and angrily throws it back down on the floor. "I hate your beer! I hate it when you're mean!"*

"You little brat!" Dad grabs Henry. "I'll show you 'mean!'"

Having feelings disregarded is one thing, but challenging reality by expressing feelings can be downright dangerous emotionally, if not physically. Wise kids learn to dumb down or stuff their feelings when expressing them causes trouble.

Not only should kids learn that feelings are important clues that tell them what they need, they also need help developing tools to deal with those feelings.

Nine-year-old Sally stomped in the door after school and threw her books down on the chair.

Mom looked up. "What's wrong?"

"Chip tripped me when I got off the bus." She took a breath. "And that's not all. He's been poking me when the bus driver isn't looking and calling me names. I hate it and I hate him!"

"Tell me a little more about what happened."

Sally described behaviors that had gone on for some time.

Mom said, "I don't blame you for being mad! That's no way to treat another human being, especially you. Want to figure out a way to get him to stop?"

"If I hit him, he'll just hit me back harder."

"I was thinking of something more creative," said Mom. "What about saying something that takes him by surprise."

"I could do that," said Sally. She narrowed her eyes. "But what?"

Mom said the first thing that came to her mind. "How about calmly and firmly saying to Chip the next time he puts you down, 'Chip, you've got whipped cream in your rocks.' Then move away from him. Don't wait around for what he'll say."

Sally practiced a few of her own lines and when she came home from school a couple of days later. "Mom! It worked!"

"What worked?" Mom had forgotten Sally's plan,

"Chip shoved me today and I told him, 'Chip, you've got worms in your toes' and he just stood there. I just walked away and he didn't know what to do." Sally's smile said everything.

It's hard to stick up for yourself if you have developed a high tolerance for being dismissed or discounted. Once you're alert to what's going on, there's still the matter of deciding what to do about it.

One thing is certainly true. Engaging in a futile game of who's right about your feelings is out of the question. Your feelings are your feelings and they tell what is true for you. They have their own validity with major emphasis on the word *validity*!

Numbing out can be a perfectly legitimate survival strategy, but waking yourself up to the system of senses you were born with can make life so much richer.

Needs? What Needs?

Feelings open the door to knowing what we need. This is part of my story.

Having covered over my feelings for so long, I could intellectually acknowledge I had them but I absolutely didn't realize that I'd numbed them so much–not until I took the Minnesota Multiphasic Personality Inventory (MMPI) and was mortified to learn my anger scale score was high, high, high. My feelings had me and I wasn't happy about it. That, and more, is what urged me into therapy.

Everything went fine the first few sessions, maybe because I used the word "Fine" in reply to so many "How are you doings?" Then the therapist asked me what I thought I needed. She must have seen my blank stare because that's how I felt — blank. I paused to figure out what to say, "I need to be a good mother."

Her voice scooped up like a slide whistle. "Yes?"

I got it. She was asking for more, "I need to be a good wife and daughter."

"Yes, I'm sure you do." Pause. I was plumb out of needs.

She went on. "What you're telling me is that it's important for you to be responsible, but what do YOU need?"

I still drew a blank. I had no idea what she was talking about.

She saved me from the empty hole of my own unknowing. "I'd like you to start a list of what you need. Please bring it to our next session."

I was stuck. Then I got the brilliant idea to call a friend who lived half-way across the country. "You've known me for a while and I'm having trouble with a list I'm supposed to be making. Will you tell me something you think I need?"

It didn't take her long to come up with my list-starter. "By watching you over time, I think you need to feel you are on the leading edge of some new learning. That's when you seem happiest." Short pause.

"You're right!" Greatly relieved to have a need, I saw an avenue of need-exploration I had never considered. The next thing I added to my list was this: I need to have a certain amount of change going on in my life. There! That was number 2.

Thirty years later, I'm still making and revising that list. After all, if I don't know what I need, how can I see to getting my needs met? If I can't be clear about what I need, but still expect others to see and satisfy them, I will be disappointed. And if I don't get my needs met, then what? I'm a less resilient, more stale, and less fun person to be around.

The important conclusion is this. The information that feelings provide is crucial to knowing what I need. Knowing what my needs are is crucial to meeting them. Meeting them is central to my quality of life. The better care I take of myself, the better care I can take of others.

I offer you peace. I offer you love. I offer you friendship.
I see your beauty. I hear your need. I feel your feelings.
My wisdom flows from the Highest Source. I salute that
Source in you. Let us work together for unity and love.

Mahatma Gandhi

> **NEW RULE 3: Pay attention to your**
> **feelings. Acknowledge your feelings**
> **and use the information they provide**
> **to identify what you need.**

NOW WHAT? Replacing the Ignore Feelings Rule

Reclaiming Feelings and Needs

Is it even possible to restore buried feelings? Yes, of course. Whether numbed, hidden, or set aside, feelings are present because they are inherently part of the safety system you were born with. Although shriveled, they can be restored to their rightful place of providing the data that calls your attention to what you need. You are the one who has the privilege of bringing your feelings out of hiding, carefully breathing them back into their full, rich capacity.

What All People Need

My favorite review of what people need, which I've shortened and paraphrased below, is simple and inclusive, and it has proven its relevance over time. The list originally appeared in Gershen Kaufman and Lev Raphael's book *The Dynamics of Power: Building a Competent Self.*

Need for relationship

The need for relationship is probably the most fundamental need. Through reciprocal interest expressed over time, along with shared experiences of trust, a sense of security about a relationship gradually evolves. *Such a condition of mutuality conveys to each participant that their relationship is real, honest, and mutually valued. It is through such a relationship that we feel genuinely understood, secure in the knowledge of being loved as a separate person in our own right and wanted for ourselves. Each comes to feel that their relationship truly is wanted by the other and feels special to the other.*

Far too frequently in this culture, individuals emerge into adulthood feeling their need for relationship is dangerous at some level. Yet the call to be connected to one who loves you and who will be the one who cares for you always, moves us on in spite of

---

* The human needs as presented here are gleaned mainly from the writings of Dr. Kaufman, with Lev Raphael, as they appeared in *Dynamics of Power: Building a Competent Self* in 1983. In 1991, the current and revised edition, *Dynamics of Power: Fighting Shame & Building Self-Esteem* was published by Schenkman Books, Inc., Rochester, NY. The italicized words in this section are from the Kaufman and Raphael book.

our fears. The cultural call to be independent and self-sufficient conflicts with the need-for-relationship part of us.

Need for touching, need for holding

At certain times, wanting to be held may be motivated by a need for bodily contact or bodily warmth per se. *At other times, physical holding is a natural response to emotional need or distress. When emotional hurts motivate the need for physical comforting, holding communicates not so much affection as protection and security...the basis for developing trust.* Daily expressions of affection through touching or hugging are vital in the course of living and become the means of replenishing our emotional stores.

Touching or holding, while certainly pleasurable, is not inherently sexual. In our culture, there is widespread confusion about physical holding inevitably being connected to sex. To some, having sex *is the only way* to be nurtured. Many of us carry a sense of shame about this natural, universally experienced need for touch.

Need for identification

The need to identify is the wish to assimilate an aspect of another as our own. The process of identification begins with our parents and older siblings, and it extends to our teachers, heroes, and mentors. We identify in order to emulate those we admire, to feel the oneness—a sense of belonging—and to enhance our sense of inner power in the process. "He's like me; I'm like him." Experiences of identification become needed at critical times to provide support, strength, and healing. *Whenever we feel a need for direction, having a person we identify with means we have someone available as a guide, enabling us to navigate situations where we are uncertain or that we find threatening.* We are never alone.

Need for differentiation

We need to be separate persons from those with whom we have identified, differentiating ourselves as unique individuals by developing our own beliefs, interests, values, and skills as we acknowledge our gifts as well as our limitations.

Need to nurture

We experience the need to give to others, to nurture and put something back into the world.

Need for affirmation

We yearn to be seen and openly admired for the unique individual we are. We need to feel that *who we are, the inner person, is both worthwhile and valued.* By having someone significant provide that affirmation for us in a sustained way, we learn how to give it to ourselves.

Need for power

We have a natural human need for personal power. We need to feel in charge of our lives. We need to believe that no matter what happens, we can handle it, even if we handle it by declaring we *can't* handle it and reaching out for help. We need to feel effective. We need to feel a sense of our unique competence.

If early life experiences of humiliation and/or powerlessness have been excessive or prolonged, we tend to hone our adjustment skills. Children who experience untrustworthy care understandably think that in order to stay alive, they have to figure out a way to be in charge of getting what they need. How? By finding whatever works to keep others within their circle of influence. Be super-nice. Be super-helpful. Be super-passive. Be super-annoying and naughty. Always in hopes of getting what they need from others without having to ask directly. Paradoxically, after doing whatever works to get what they need, they also have difficulty believeing they deserve to have their needs met.

There are those who use feelings themselves to get what they need. Molly pretends to be sad if that works to get Derek to take care of her. Juan puffs up his anger when he wants someone else to back down. Harry pretends he's devastated when Ivy won't go fishing with him. Feelings have such integrity on their own, that to use them to manipulate others is a case of crying wolf. Cody should rightly have a healthy fear of driving 80 miles an hour on a snow-packed road to impress his friend. It would be best for Carrie's health if she declined to take a ride with a stranger when she felt a stab of fear that warned her of danger.

Our capacity to feel and know what we need is crucial to the quality of our life experience. A rule that says we should ignore our feelings is foolish and endangers our health.

There are two ways to live your life; one as if nothing is a miracle, and the other as if everything is a miracle.

Albert Einstein

Verbal Intimacy

Intimacy is based on self-disclosure.[14] Telling the truth as found in our feelings and expecting to be heard and, hopefully, understood is the crux of getting closer to another person. If we avoid conflict, the opportunity to develop more trust in our relationships passes us by. Relationships suffer when we stop learning more about one another.

Here's how that tends to work: I tell you something and watch to see how you receive it. I have taken a risk and you met me with understanding. I trust you more. I feel closer to you. I start with a fairly safe disclosure. If that goes well, I'm encouraged to share something a little deeper. And so on. This assumes I have become familiar enough with my history, what it meant to me, and maybe even how it's helped me or held me back from knowing myself. Creating intimacy through progressive sharing requires me to be well-acquainted with myself so I can share something more than just vital statistics. Sharing the effects of those "statistics" makes us a lot more interesting than the facts alone.

In his early 20s, Carlos wanted to know more about his dad. He knew him as a dad but he wanted to know more about him as a man and a person. Carlos felt he'd missed something in that arena. Carlos's therapist recommended he satisfy his curiosity by asking his dad for some stories about his own growing up. How did he experience and understand his life? What were his challenges? What was he proud of? Did he have regrets?

Carlos had his reservations about probing his dad's history. He was known as a "private" person. Nevertheless, over a spaghetti dinner, Carlos asked, "What kinds of things did you and your father do together?" That seemed like a non-threatening place to start.

His dad replied, "I liked it a lot when he took me fishing. I remember that on this one big lake, we caught a lot of fish and he teased me because I caught the biggest one."

"What was your dad like?" asked Carlos.

"What do you mean? He was a dad."

"What did you admire about him?"

"He liked to tell stories and he was fun to be around–except when he wasn't."

"Oh. Tell me what you remember about his being fun and not fun."

Carlos's dad thought for a minute and said, "Oh, you know. The usual stuff. He was a hard worker."

Carlos continued asking questions geared to learning more about his dad. It became clear that Dad stuck to describing situations, but never how they impacted him. His stories could be interesting, but his very private dad wouldn't say much about how anything affected him. "I didn't find out much about what had meaning in his life," said Carlos.

The Old Rules make verbal intimacy difficult because of the many ways they cause us to defend ourselves. Keeping emotional distance from others serves a self-protective function and it takes courage to soften our defenses and begin seeing ourselves as whole, as imperfect, and as a person worth knowing and worth knowing better.

Slipping the Hooks, Making the Turn

If you undertake the process of becoming better acquainted with your feelings, pick one activity, the one that speaks to you first. See what you learn about yourself. It is your choice to believe and operate by the Old Rule or the New Rule. It is your option to experiment with the replacement rule and discover what works for you.

- Observe without judgment what you are feeling in any instance. Then look at what triggered the feeling. You don't need to draw conclusions. Just notice compassionately what you're feeling. Notice and think about the connection between what you're feeling and what you need.
- After you've observed your feelings, ask yourself how much you think you trust your feelings to tell you the truth. Observe whether your feelings are a reliable signal to what's happening in your interactions. Pretend your assessment is accurate! You are correct! After all, you don't need to argue with anyone about whether your feelings are right or wrong!
- Use the Feelings and Needs worksheet in Appendix D to practice letting your feelings guide you to a positive response.
- Keep a feelings journal. Write about current or past experiences that have strong emotions connected to them. Let yourself know where in your body you felt the feeling. What was the feeling telling you? Continue being

curious about your experiences of getting information from your feelings.

- Begin making your personal List of Needs.
- Consult the affirmations relative to this chapter in Appendix B.
- If you are a researcher by nature, do a search for topics like affect theory, emotional intelligence, feelings, and human needs to extend your understanding of how respecting feelings contributes to an over-all sense of life satisfaction.
- You deserve to find a therapist if you need one. This idea has traction for those of us who felt we have had to do life by ourselves and not ask or expect help from others. Strongly consider breaking that nonsensical rule.

Your feelings have a lot to do with intimacy and the satisfaction that is possible in your relationships. Feelings are the pathway that takes you to yourself. To genuinely love someone, you really have to know them.

Carol Gilligan

The Ghosts of Unresolved Grief

Part of the shroud that can drape over a person's life is almost mystical. It consists of the losses in our lives that we haven't fully grieved. Losses not fully grieved compose an unnamed, deadening pall that lies outside our conscious awareness. That pall can hang around in a way that arrests the benefits of our emotional nature.

There may be many factors that impact our grieving. Maybe we don't want to acknowledge how much we loved, appreciated, resented, or needed another because it involves more emotional pain than we're up for. Maybe we heed the voices who say *get on with your life* and we take that to mean we should be over our grief about our loss. Maybe we don't have someone who will listen to our stories about the one who has left and the important meaning they had in our lives. Maybe we carry old messages about the authenticity or acceptability of sad feelings.

Maybe our loss happened before we could express ourselves with language. Pre-verbal losses get into every cell of our bodies at a time before we're able to cognitively acknowledge them with conscious grieving. Maybe our loss occurred at a time when others around us parked their grief, or having so much of it themselves, they couldn't help us with our feelings about ours. And maybe ungrieved losses have piled up in our families for decades, even generations, and no one ever talks about them because they're too painful or shameful. Averting attention from these losses is a way to unintentionally pretend the losses don't matter. But they did, and they do, and they have a way of hanging around in a powerful, but unseen, way.

Grieving is a part of living. Vinny "lost" his keys and experienced the full cycle of grief quickly. "No, it can't be true! I left them on the counter!" Then "I don't have time to look for them" followed by extreme frustration as he looked everywhere. "Maybe I'll have to call and cancel my date." He stopped and took a deep breath. "Oh yeah, check the pocket of the jacket I wore yesterday." And there they were. Note that he didn't find the keys until he'd got to the point of acceptance that they were, indeed, lost. A full grief cycle in under 2 minutes.

Whatever comes into our lives also leaves. A baby is welcomed to the world by joyful parents. A coming in. Parents lose sleep, flexibility of schedule, and a guest bedroom. A loss. Gains and losses happen every day.

The really big ones that matter a lot are full circle grieving projects. Sometimes the big losses go back to another generation or more and remain as a burden carried by families that don't ever notice that someone else's unresolved grief has been silently passed on to them. It's never too late to recognize and account for those losses in order to release them and travel further.[15]

Letitia stopped short at hearing that grief can last for generations.

My mom was orphaned and grew up with any relative who would take her. A few years before she died, she told me something that made so much sense. She said, "For five years, one of them did all kinds of sexual things to me. I hated it, but I didn't know what to do. In those days, you didn't tell anyone, ever." I felt so sorry for her.

Now I understand why she never touched me or my brother or my sister. When my sister told my mother she loved her, my mother said, "Ditto." I absolutely know she loved us, but she couldn't say it....or give us hugs.

She was confused between the words and deeds of love, and so was I, as it turns out. I'm married, but I have to say, I keep my distance from men, except from my husband. I thought I had my own reasons because a roomer who lived on the third floor was sexually inappropriate with me when I was 10. The second time he tried it, I refused and got away quickly–and told my dad. He went straight to the third floor and was back in five minutes. Later I found out he had told the guy he had to be moved out by sundown or he'd call the police.

You asked me what I thought about unresolved grief. Now I see that I've carried a grief about missing affection from my mom, and I've thought all this time it was my fault.

Letitia ended her story by saying, *"I hope you tell this story in your book. It would be a way to honor Mother."*

Moving On

Above all, be patient with yourself. It's taken a long time and many experiences to install the unwanted stuff embedded in the Old Rules. None of us knows how to turn our understanding and behavior around on a dime. It takes time. And by the way, you'll never do it perfectly. Perfection isn't the issue. Persistence is. Taking good care of what you need is.

There's a reason we've been given the ability to feel. Feelings are meant to keep us safe and alive. They respond to the realities of life and give us information about the dynamics around us, even before we have any understanding of language. As we grow, a robust awareness of how our contexts are affecting us makes possible the full measure of experiencing life richly. Disregarding feelings is tantamount to disregarding life.

Next, we will examine another rule that complicates relationships. It's the practice of using deception to hide shame, even when we don't need to.

The greatest degree of inner tranquility comes from the development of love and compassion. The more we care for the happiness of others, the greater is our own sense of well-being.

Tenzin Gyatso, 14th Dalai Lama

CHAPTER SEVEN

OLD RULE 4: KEEP SECRETS

Do not raise the issue or ask questions
about whatever might jeopardize the status quo.

He who has the secret, has the power.

Catherine Bateson

WHAT? The Meaning of the Old Keep Secrets Rule

A general felt sense of insecurity is common when we fear there is something wrong with us, or even just not quite right. One of the ways we hide our inadequacies from the eyes that might see and expose them is to keep secrets.

Some secrets require lying, others don't. They all require holding back certain pieces of factual information. Most secrets are toxic. They cause damage and pain to self and others.

Keeping secrets is inevitable when a family wants to be seen as being and doing right. A break or violation in what is socially acceptable behavior might reveal a problem the family is not ready to solve. And they risk losing status if the secret becomes known to others.

A neurosis is a secret that you don't know you are keeping.
                                                            Kenneth Tynan

---

Reasons to Keep Secrets and Tell Lies

The three biggest reasons to keep secrets and tell lies are: 1) to protect the self and our interests, 2) to protect someone else, and 3) to avoid unwanted consequences.

Protection of self and one's interests

Having engaged in behavior we're not proud of, most of us wish to prevent any unwelcome scrutiny of what we've done. We are highly motivated to uphold the image of ourselves as okay persons.

Becky, 15, was having sex regularly with her 18-year-old boyfriend. She knew her parents would "have a fit" if they found out. When her dad became suspicious and asked directly why she'd come home late three times that week, Becky lied and said she and a friend were studying algebra and just didn't realize she was past her school night curfew. Becky asked her best friend to corroborate her lie, if that became necessary.

In telling this story years later, Becky said, "I can't believe I got away with it, but Mom and Dad were too preoccupied with their own stuff to notice. Anyway, I don't think they really wanted to find out what I was doing. Except for keeping me in chains, I'm sure they didn't know what to do to stop me. I'm not proud of what I did! I really didn't get away with it because to this day, every time I think of it, I get a knot in the middle of my stomach."

There's a fine line between privacy and keeping secrets. Becky was 15 and still learning about taking good care of herself. Later reflections on her 15-year-old behavior tells us she considered the incident one of lying to keep a secret. It wasn't just about privacy alone. Some things are nobody else's business because we are the only ones affected by what we withhold. *They don't need to know how much money I make.* That's privacy.

Protection of someone else

For centuries, the stakes for exposing a problem have been high. It is, after all, seen as in the best interests of family safety to maintain a community presence of acceptability. In Jane Austen's novel *Pride and Prejudice*, when one of four daughters runs off with an army officer, her family is thrown into despair. When the daughter's miscreant behavior becomes known, it means the other three daughters' chances of marrying well have been dashed.

Secret-keeping is often justified when the information is regarded as hurtful to another person. A rightful question to ask is *by keeping the secret, whose interests are being served?*

- The patient is not told his illness is terminal.
- Social workers don't tell an adult adoptee seeking information that she was a product of rape.
- The family refers to a nephew's shooting of his father as "the unfortunate incident."
- Fred doesn't tell his best friend George he's seen George's wife with another man.
- Eric doesn't tell his friend they can't play at his house after school because his mother might be drunk.
- Justine doesn't tell her partner that she knows her mother is mentally ill.

Hiding a family member's addiction or dependency on something that is seen as necessary or laudable like work, food, church, exercise, charity work, or sports is among the most difficult to acknowledge or call out as a problem. The very definition of an addiction means that a person has a primary relationship with something other than with relationships that are supposed to top the list, like family and friends. How can family members acknowledge, even to themselves, the hurt of playing second fiddle?

Everyone who protects others by not telling the truth has their own reason. The stakes may be too high, or the one who would reveal the secret may fear being made *wrong*. In these cases, someone benefits from keeping the secret in the name of protecting others. The experience of Sharon, a recovering alcoholic, illustrates the point.

When I spilled a drink on the carpet at a party and was on my hands and knees sopping it up with a towel, I remember making a joke by saying, "You'd think I was an alcoholic." The voice of a guy standing nearby softly and gently said, "Well, maybe you are." I wish I knew who the guy was, because I'd like to thank him. He's the first person I heard tell the truth. My husband and I both had problems with drinking. When I fell down the stairs and broke my leg, I wouldn't let him take me to the emergency room until I sobered up and he, of course, agreed. That's how deluded we were. Although I thought I was close to my mother and two sisters, they never said anything to me about my drinking. This perfect stranger said what my heart knew–and shortly after that, I wound up going to treatment. I am so grateful! I wish I could thank him.

Nothing makes us so lonely as our secrets.

Paul Tournier

Perhaps every secret has two losers or more. And maybe not. Allie learned of her ex-husband's infidelities shortly before his death. She decided not to tell her adult children. "I don't want to contaminate how they think of their father." Who's to say if that's the best choice? So often when we withhold information we think would be hurtful, the ones we've withheld the information from at some level know it already.

It's difficult to assess what purpose sharing the information about a father or mother's infidelity posthumously would serve. Respect and cohesion among family members might follow such a revelation, or resentment and judgment might cloud their positive memories. How are their lives affected by knowing the secret? By not knowing the secret?

Avoiding unwanted consequences

Secrets and lies are commonly used to avoid the consequences of having our behavior known to others. Whether we're trying to steer around the loss of face or reputation or the fear of punishment, when we're not proud of what we've done, we want to avoid the subject. An early step in recovery of nearly everything is the challenge to come clean, to get real.

At 13, Jon was given advertising circulars he was supposed to deliver along with the newspapers to customers on his route. His mom asked how he was managing to carry the heavy newspaper bag. "Just fine," he said.

Six weeks later, Mom found stacks of circulars hidden in the garage. Jon blew up when his secret was discovered.

Jon's rage is a pretty common reaction to having been "found out." For Jon, the greatest consequence of Mom's discovery was disappointing someone who loved him. He also disappointed himself because his actions didn't represent who he believed himself to be.

Let's acknowledge here that there are times when lying, or keeping the secret to yourself, is helpful.

An eighth grader went back to his elementary school to visit his sixth-grade teacher. "Mrs. Hayes, remember how you taught us it's important to tell the truth."

"Yes."

"Well, I told a lie."

"No kidding! Are you going to tell me what it was?"

"Well, three neighborhood guys were planning to do something I didn't want to get involved with after we got off the bus from school. I told them I couldn't go with them because my mom told me she'd tip my fish tank over on the front lawn if I hadn't cleaned it by the time she got home from work."

"You mean that wasn't true?

"No. It was a lie."

"Did the lie hurt anyone else? Did it hurt you? Did it help you handle a delicate situation?"

"No, no, and yes."

"It seems to me you lied as a strategy to keep yourself in a place you wanted to be. I wouldn't be for making lying a habit, but as long as it didn't harm you or anyone else but helped instead, it's totally permissible in my book," the teacher said with a small smile.

What we call "little white lies" are also useful at times when our opinion is solicited and telling the truth isn't really the issue. In proudly showing his best friend his new boat, Edgar exclaimed, "Don't you think I've got the best boat on the market?" Or Georgia, delighted with something she sees in the store window, says, "Don't you just love this?" We can all be happy for the joy of others, but these occasions don't call for brutal honesty. How about "It's easy to see how much you love it" or "I'm glad you're so happy with your choice" or "It's not my thing, but I'm happy you're happy."

SO WHAT? Some Effects of KEEPING SECRETS

Secrets Have Consequences

Beth had a special relationship with her sister, Jessie, who was seven years older. Beth wasn't the tag-along sister; she was a bring-along kind of kid. One day, absolutely everything changed. Beth's mom and dad brought home a new baby. "You have a new sister. We're adopting this sweet little girl!" No one helped Beth prepare for this event.

Surprised by the addition of baby Emma, Beth soon found that her treasured older sister now spent her time and attention on the new baby, leaving Beth to wonder what was wrong with her.

Beth was also surprised by a secret her mother insisted she keep. "If you ever tell Emma she's adopted, you will ruin her life."

Much later as a 20-something, Beth confronted her mother about the lie and again, her mother threatened her about not telling because of all the damage she would do.

It wasn't until the "baby" was 18 and needed to produce a birth certificate that she discovered her family's fabrication. In fact, Beth's older sister was actually her birthmother. Emma lost no time in confronting Jessie. The two of them agreed it was their secret to keep.

It was years later before they finally told Beth. "But don't tell Mom," they said. "She doesn't know we know."

Beth was flooded with feelings about the years of living in a family and community where other people knew and she didn't. For too many years, she'd felt "odd woman out." She'd assumed there was something wrong with her that resulted in her feeling left out and only "sort of" connected. "God knows, I didn't tell anybody about the adoption, so I never understood why the relationship between my sisters, my mom, and me felt so weird."

With their now common knowledge, Beth, Jessie, and Emma were free to have an open relationship with one another. They shared their common knowledge of the secret as a kind of bonding intimacy between them. It was as if a wall had been taken down. And the three of them never did tell their mom they all knew the secret. "Tiptoeing around the truth. Screening what you say so you don't slip and say the forbidden thing. At best, you could say we had years of a very edited relationship," said Beth.

In telling this story, Beth spoke of many years feeling like *The Little Match Girl*. A shivering girl in tattered clothing, standing outside in the cold and peering through the window to watch the happy, loving family together around the warm glow of the fireplace and asking herself. "Who are these people? I know I belong with them, but..."

Secrets are never innocuous. Secrets have consequences. Secrets affect other people's lives and our own.

Keep It in the Family

Every family has secrets. There are secrets that the family recognizes as needing to be secret but no one talks about. There are secrets that the family acknowledges among themselves, but doesn't want people outside the family to know. There's a reason why secrets and lies go together. Keeping secrets requires lying. Lying to others and lying to oneself. Few of us boast about keeping the kind of secrets that we think reflect badly on our families. No, even *that* is a secret.

Facts seem to have their own energy. When an event occurs, it is real, even if we don't consciously have information about it. There is a place in the field of energy around us that is reserved for whatever actually happens. At some level, we all have knowledge of the existence of the truth. Most people keep themselves from acknowledging a secret out loud, but when the secret is finally revealed to them, "I knew it!" is a common response. So is "I don't believe you!"

Lying is a cooperative act. Someone agrees to believe the lie.

Pamela Meyer

Another Look at Secrets

Keeping secrets creates distance in relationships. It usually happens gradually and without intention. The distance widens slowly, until one day the emotional gulf between two people is wide and deep. Secrets don't make good building blocks.

Jamie and her husband, Ralph, both had secrets they kept. Ralph didn't want Jamie to know he'd wanted to marry someone else and that his fiancée had broken their engagement. Jamie didn't want Ralph to know she'd not been as popular in school and not nearly as confident as she pretended to be.

After 20 years in a marriage that was growing more and more distant, one day Jamie's mother-in-law slipped and let the cat out of Ralph's bag. "Why didn't he tell me that?" She felt a mixture of anger and regret. "If marriage means being honest – not cruel, but honest – then Ralph's telling me that early on could have made a big difference. He didn't trust me. I probably would have been jealous, but we could have worked through that."

Jamie got very quiet. "And maybe he sensed my low opinion of myself and didn't think he could risk it."

Could it be possible to reconstitute her dwindling relationship with Ralph? She was hopeful more honest sharing would help. But after years of distance caused by what they didn't know about one another, would this be a case of too little, too late?

If we're human and if we're breathing, there's a lot to learn about ourselves. In a shame-based family, learning about our true selves is not so easy. The old rules encourage us to stay away from who we truly are, for fear of exposing our supposedly defective selves to humiliation. But if intimacy is based on self-disclosure, we're the only ones who can compassionately find out who's under the façade. If we pasted together a picture of ourselves derived from how we were treated, defending ourselves from being seen is second nature. We all have experiences, but no one told us that we are *not* our experiences. Our experiences need not define us.

Let's say Jamie shares something about herself with Ralph, perhaps something really safe at first. She waits to see how Ralph treats her disclosure. If he treats her with respect and compassion, Jamie is likely to trust Ralph more and feel closer to him. However, if Ralph ignores, actively denies, or humiliates Jamie for what she discloses, she's not apt to feel emotionally safe with him and their relationship probably won't go to the level of closeness they really want.[16] This process, repeated over and over again, helps us discover not only our put-away selves, but the self of another.

A destructive secret kept, keeps its power to destroy.
A destructive secret shared, loses all its power.

Edward Trembley

A Cautionary Tale

Our temperaments cause us to process data differently. What appears to be secret-keeping to an extrovert may just be internal processing time to an introvert.

A mom and her 13-year-old son, Tim, met with a counselor. Mom wanted help to figure out why Tim seemed to be so "uncooperative" and "disrespectful." For Tim's part, he didn't get why she was so upset.

Mom said, "When I ask Tim a question, he doesn't answer me right away."

Looking at Mom, the counselor asked, "And you take his slowness to respond as a sign of disrespect?"

Bottom line: Mom was an acknowledged extrovert and her son, a pretty dedicated introvert. Their styles are part of their natures. In discussing how their styles affected their relationship, Mom said, "When I ask you a question, Tim, and you don't answer me right away, I think you're dissing me and I get ticked."

The counselor looked at Tim. "Will you tell your mother what's happening on your end of her questions?"

"I'm thinking," said Tim. "She wants a quick answer from me and I have to take it through my head before I can give her an

answer. I'm not just being a butt. And I'm not trying to make something up."

Although it seemed to his mom that Tim was being secretive, the acknowledgement of this difference reminded her to check out Tim's responses and gave both a chance to remove a stumbling block in their communication.

The Best Kept Secret

There must be a placeholder for truth. If something really happened, there must be a space for it somewhere.

A family may suffer from a lurking legacy of lies and cover-ups going back generations. Some families find ways to keep blind eyes and deaf ears to painful histories. Abuse, promiscuity, criminal behavior, mental illness – anything that the family sees as shameful. Others are clueless about what happened and how it was covered up. However, if someone, sometime, discovers another piece of the legacy puzzle, a new depth of understanding is possible. More of reality is open to scrutiny and of course, understanding. A prior sense of incompleteness is relieved.

A wise family therapist has said that a family system locked into a generations-old pattern of keeping secrets begs for someone to "spit in their soup." The system needs disturbing, in hopes that the long-repressed truth will leak out and give the family a chance to confront and heal old wounds. Truth pushes to get through deception.

The slogan on my favorite lapel button says, "Say what

everyone is thinking." A sequel might be "Say what everyone knows but doesn't realize they know until they actually hear it said."

Yes, truth seeks the light of day. The shroud of secrecy begs to be addressed, not avoided. How can we change what we don't even recognize?

You can't have peace until you have all the pieces.

Troy Dunn

An Effect on the Secret-keeper

Whether they are kept to protect ourselves or others, secrets of commission or omission both have an impact on the secret-keeper. Lexie's story is one of active lying.

"My mother phoned to ask what I was doing on Saturday. I told her I had to go to a workshop. It was a lie. My daughter and I were looking forward to spending the weekend shopping in a nearby city and honestly, I didn't want my mother to go along."

The least of the consequences for Lexie was having to tip-toe around her mother to be sure she didn't give away the secret after the fact. "I had to swear my daughter to secrecy, which made her complicit in the lie. And, frankly, I felt crappy about the whole thing. I damaged my picture of who I am. It would have been hard, but in the long run, so much easier on me if I had simply told Mother that Allison and I wanted some mother-daughter time."

On the other hand, Rebecca's story is an example of omission, withholding, or passive lying.

Rebecca was in her 50's when she came face to face with information that had been withheld from her. She'd grown up an only child adopted when she was a week old through Catholic Social Services. "I was a good girl in a happy home. At my first communion, I shocked myself when I broke out sobbing because I had to say I would honor my father and mother. I'm still not altogether clear what that was about. I must have been thinking about my unknown birth parents. How was I to honor them when I didn't even know who they were? How could I pledge something I couldn't fulfill?"

As a teen, Rebecca was drawn to the youth group at her local synagogue and wound up attending services many Friday nights. She was fascinated by everything Jewish. In her mid-30s, she decided to convert to Judaism. It was after her conversion that she initiated a search for her birth parents. "I found out that both my birth mother and birth father were Jewish. My birth mother had been sent to another town during her pregnancy, and in a series of maneuvers I still don't understand, I was placed with a Catholic family even though my birth mother had asked I be placed with a Jewish family. It was a great relief to know the truth because my attraction to the synagogue and all things Jewish didn't make sense to anyone, not even me."

In her early 50s, supported by her adoptive parents, husband, and four children, Rebecca celebrated her bat mitzvah.

Rebecca's reaction to having her origins withheld from her was to question what other information may have been hidden from her. "What else haven't I been told? I didn't know if I could trust them about anything if they'd withhold the truth from me like they did." But her parents were never told they were given a Jewish girl so how were they to make sense of what Rebecca needed as she was growing up?

We dance round in a ring and suppose, but the secret sits in the middle and knows.

Robert Frost

NEW RULE 4: Tell your truth in the most respectful and likely receivable way, after first recognizing your own.

NOW WHAT? Replacing the Keeping Secrets Rule

A good way to get a handle on the truth is to begin putting together "body hits," those feelings in the gut that you don't necessarily ascribe to anything in particular at the time they happen, but taken together, are hard to overlook. Alert! Truth may be hanging around, trying to get your attention.

Truth may be true only for the person declaring it. We all see what we see through our personal lenses or frames of reference. Arguing about two truths to determine whose is right leads nowhere.

Here's an example of someone's truth spoken in the most likely receivable way.

I'm worried about you when you're drinking because you fell down the front steps last week and then argued with Uncle Ben when he asked you to give him the car keys. I was scared to death something bad might happen. I'm sorry I didn't speak up. This isn't the first time. I love you and I want you to get help to stop drinking. I'm going to an Alanon meeting day after tomorrow.

Slipping the Hooks, Making the Turn

- We've all said or done, or not said and left undone, something we regret. Although it was never acknowledged, it stays on in the heart as a piece of unfinished business. Think of two examples of each kind of lie from your past: An active lie (to avoid consequences) and a passive lie (whithholding information).

- Own your own truth and let go of trying to convince others your truth is right. This gives others the opportunity to own theirs.

- Use the Secrets and Lies worksheet in Appendix D to discover more about their impact.

- Speaking with someone about a hard-to-speak-about-truth can be more easiy done if you keep a few things in mind. Think of a piece of unfinished business whose residual effects are complicating a relationship. Then ease the way by using the following tips:
  - o Ask the other person if they are willing to talk with you. Set a time convenient to both of you and a place relatively free from distractions.

- o When you meet, you may want to thank the other person for being willing to talk with you. Remember this is *your* need.
- o Take the other person back to a specific situation or incident so both of you remember the same context.
- o Take care to begin your sentences with "I" and own your need to have the conversation. This tends to reduce defensiveness at the get-go. Avoid using global words like "never" and "always."
- o Talk about your feelings about what happened or what was said.
- o Be as calm and non-judgmental as you know how to be.
- o If you're hoping to repair, restore or complete this relationship, say so.
- o Listen to what the other person says. Ask questions if you need to, but only to be clear about what the other person is thinking or feeling.
- o Make a new agreement for moving forward.
- Do no cruelty. This is an exercise in cleaning up the past. Brenda Ueland[17] believed only two rules are needed to guide a sensible and upright life. They are **Tell the truth, and Do no cruelty**.
- Think of a time when you kept a secret and a time you told a difficult-to-tell truth. These questions may help you understand who might benefit from telling lies or withholding the truth.
  - o Am I, or have I been, protecting myself or protecting another person?

o   If the other person knew what I know, might they use it to improve their quality of life?

o   Will telling what I know result in harm to myself or another?

o   Am I projecting my needs and beliefs onto others? Is what I'm saying about another also true of me?

o   How do I benefit from telling the secret?

o   Am I willing to apologize? Am I willing to listen?

o   Am I willing to handle the consequences of telling the lie?

o   Is spreading a rumor a way for me to have a feeling of intimacy or importance?

As you recognize how you have been drawn into keeping secrets, be gentle with yourself and admire the empathy and sensitivity you have and are continuing to develop.

A way to tell a secret, any secret, is made possible at <u>www.postsecret.com</u>

If you don't want it printed, don't let it happen.

Aspen Daily News

Moving On

There isn't one of us who has NOT been secretive. It's part of defending ourselves from being exposed as having made a mistake, or out of fear that we *are* the mistake. Keeping toxic secrets feeds our shame by affirming a need to defend or hide who we are. Beings who have come clean about harmful past secrets free themselves of needing to hide and pretend.

Beings who apologize, accept responsibility, and do some kind of restitution lighten the psychic drag on their lives. When they do these things they feel more powerful, for strangely enough, by keeping toxic secrets, they give their integrity and therefore, their power, away.

Next, we'll explore one of the ramifications of Rules 1-4, especially on our determination to be reliable and expect reliability from others.

If you don't want to be deceived, you have
to know what you're hungry for.

Pamela Meyer[18]

CHAPTER EIGHT

OLD RULE 5: BE UNCLEAR AND UNACCOUNTABLE

Don't communicate clearly.

Be wary of commitments, promises, and agreements.

It is not only what we do, but also what we do not do, for which we are accountable.

Moliere

WHAT? The Meaning of the Old Be Unclear and Unaccountable Rule

If we grew up with the Old Rules, and since human beings hunger for a level of certainty, having a rule that says it doesn't matter isn't helpful. We humans seem to want to know things like where our next meal is coming from, what we should do in case of fire, and who'll be there when we need help.

In the generational scheme of family organization, adults

are in charge of the safety, protection, and care of the children. In the case of workers, bosses are the responsible parties. Children and workers also have their responsibilities. In this chapter, we explore what happens when adults have a hard time being accountable for their decisions and behaviors.

We all want to know that if you say you will be there, you will be there. If you say you will do something, we want to count on your staying true to your word. We want to know that a promise made is a promise kept unless both parties re-negotiate the terms of the promise and it is re-made.

There are some promises that are not possible to fulfill for any number of valid reasons. For instance, you fail to show up at a meeting because you broke a leg. You promise your son a new bike and lose your job. That kind of interference with your commitment can be accounted for. It barely causes a ruffle. It's fixed by an acknowledgement of the "failure," followed by an apology and the making of a new contract or understanding. This tells others they can count on you. You can be trusted.

The following hard-to-believe story is just one of the lessons about the lack of accountability Ellis learned as a child.

For months before his birthday, Ellis's dad promised him a new bicycle. When the big day arrived, Ellis's dad stopped at the tavern on his way home and stayed until closing. Ellis waited in the living room for hours and finally went to bed.

The next morning, he got up early, only to be told not to bother Dad because he didn't feel well. Ellis waited with as much patience as he could muster.

Later that day, Dad finally took Ellis to the bicycle store.

Looking at the bikes in the window, Dad said, "Pick the one you like."

"That one!" Ellis pointed. It was the bike he'd had his eye on for weeks.

After a short pause, Dad said, "Okay. Time to get back home."

"What? What did he just say?" Ellis asked himself. He froze in disbelief and then collapsed into dismay. His whole body sank. He knew not to ask why he wasn't getting the bike.

This incident had been preceded by countless other times when Ellis's dad made a promise and failed to deliver. Still, with every promise, Ellis thought, *This time will be different,* but it never was. *"First I stopped hoping, then I stopped believing,"* he said.

Answerability: Being Accountable

To be accountable, we must consider the consequences of what we do. Sometimes the consequences of an action are positive, like when you do what you say you will do. In Ellis's situation, the consequences were negative, apparently not for his father, but certainly for Ellis. We don't know if or how his dad was impacted by Ellis's disappointment. If he was, that was Dad's consequence. There's a serious problem present if Ellis's dad felt absolutely no consequence of his actions.

In the following case, Kevin's behavior was unacceptable, and his consequence was logical and negative at first, though the final outcome was positive.

Kevin, 17, got a speeding ticket, which qualified him to show up at the old sandstone City Hall downtown accompanied by a parent. On the way to the meeting, Kevin told his mother that all the kids told him to get out of any consequences by making up an excuse to tell the judge. If he pulled it off, he wouldn't be assigned to attend dumb-dumb driving school...or worse, have his license suspended. "Were you driving over the speed limit?" asked his mother.

"Yes," came his reply.

"Well then. That's your story."

After listening to an hour-long lecture, the judge retreated to a bubbled glass-enclosed office at the rear of the old courtroom. One by one, the bailiff summoned each driver and parent(s) into the office. Everyone waited their turn quietly and nervously. They could hear almost every word spoken.

"This citation says you were driving while others in your car were drinking. Is that true?"

"Well, sort of," said one young man.

"Son, are you aware that the driver is responsible for law-breaking behaviors of others in the car?" asked the judge.

"Well....."

Then, a deep male voice started "sticking up" for his son. Dad took over and had a brief, if slightly exaggerated, explanation (excuse) in his son's defense.

"Son, I'm suspending your license for six months and requiring you to attend a six-week class to review the responsibilities of a driver," said the judge.

Similar situations followed.

When Kevin's turn came, the judge took his time looking over a copy of the ticket.

"Well, if this isn't something!" Mom pictured Kevin being frog-marched off to jail. The judge went on. "You're the first one today.

The officer says here that you were polite, son. And you didn't claim you were not at fault. Is that true?"

"Yes, sir," came Kevin's quiet reply.

"Well, then," dropping a portion of his sternness, "I like your show of respect to the officer and I like that you accepted your ticket, although," nodding toward his mom, "I'm pretty sure you knew she wouldn't be happy you got the ticket."

"No, sir. She wasn't."

"Have you learned your lesson then? Will you be honoring speed limits from now on?"

"Yes, sir."

"I believe you. Make it a good life," said the judge with an ever-so-slight twinkle in his eye.

Kevin and his mother exited the courtroom without saying a word. On the way to the car, Kevin sighed out his tension, smiled, and said, "That was almost a good experience."

As in the chapter on blame, the operative word here is *rectitude,* the satisfaction that comes when we have done what we perceive to be honest and true to our character. Actions have consequences. What we choose to do, or think, or believe should do no harm to others—or to ourselves.

As the Dalai Lama says, "There are no mistakes, only lessons."

SO WHAT? Some Effects of Being Unaccountable

Accountability and Self-Respect

Among the most telling consequences when someone is not accountable are those measured by the esteem lost by both parties. We don't look for ways to be considered untrustworthy. Nevertheless, we diminish ourselves in our own eyes if we fabricate, camouflage, and duck our way through life seemingly unaware of the hurt we inflict on ourselves and others. But that's what happens as we fail to acknowledge the consequences of our actions. Perhaps the greatest result of not learning from consequences is the damage done to important relationships. We teach people what to expect from us—and to what degree *they* can or cannot trust us.

A little guilt is a good thing if that guilt signals a discrepancy between who we say we are and what we do. Picture the scales of justice. On one scale is what we *say* and on the other scale, what we do. When those two scales are balanced, we are congruent. When those two scales are balanced our intentions and behaviors match.

Years ago, my mother was in a nursing home and I intended to visit her at least three times a week. If a week went by without visiting, I felt guilty. I value loyalty and compassion. My behavior didn't match my values. Guilt signalled the scales were unbalanced. I knew I could respond to the guilt by changing either my value/intention or my behavior, or both, to bring the scales back into balance. When the scales were in balance again, so was I.

The Difference between Clarity and Criticism

Criticism is often meant to be helpful. It's a common way of helping others improve their skills. For someone who is used to criticism that is demeaning, however, it's not the best way to help.

In the past, whenever Ted was discovered as having made a mistake, or having been less than perfect, he reacted defensively. For him, that meant slinking away in silence and feeling terrible about himself. Even something like *Your use of commas is inconsistent. Please check the punctuation rules and edit the chapter accordingly* was a problem. He would hear the comment as criticism instead of a helpful clarification. Now, instead of going into the place of his unworthiness, Ted is getting better at thanking the person who made the comment because he's becoming a better writer.

Ted wrote this story about himself as a boy

After watching, then "helping" his father mow the lawn, one day Ted convinced his father he knew how to mow the lawn all by himself.

His dad reminded Ted, "When you get to the tree, just swerve around it and keep going." Then he helped Ted get started and disappeared into the garage. "Come and get me when you're done," he said.

The new mower's chest swelled with confidence and pure pleasure and when he had finished the job, he could hardly wait to find Dad. "It's all done! Come and see!"

The smile of approval the boy anticipated wasn't there. "Look at the strips of grass you missed!" Dad took the mower and went back over the missed grass. "And you didn't get close enough to the fence! You said you knew how to mow!"

Ted whirled around and ran blindly into the house, slamming the door behind him.

For his part, Dad was shocked and confused. When his mom asked why Ted had slammed his door, her husband said, "I have no idea. Just leave him alone."

'That happened 30 years ago," Ted said, "Mom and I were reminiscing when she said the incident was one of those times she knew she should do or say something to help me, but had no idea what. As a kid, she'd experienced the same thing.

It helps me now to hear Mom say, "I wish I had knocked on your door. I would have made sure I re-connected with you when you were ready. I would have reassured you that I saw you as learning to be capable and hoped you'd try again. And I would have had words with your father. We both had some ancestral hand-me-downs about criticism that we needed to attend to."

As parents or as supervisors and leaders, we intend to teach, not criticize or humiliate. When dealing with behavior, humiliation by criticism doesn't talk about *behavior*, it talks about *personhood*. It says *What's wrong with you?* instead of *This part works well and that part needs shoring up in this way. Let me explain.* This gives the other person credit. It's based on a belief that when we know what we can do to do better, we do it.

The Truth About Criticism

Criticism occurs when a suggestion, comment, or correction of an undesirable or unwanted behavior is directed more at the *person* engaging in the behavior than at the behavior itself. Criticism is particularly destructive when accompanied by the look and voice of disdain. It doesn't offer *here's what you could do instead* information, only an implicit blame or exposure of the other as "bad." It is for this reason that I question the term *constructive criticism.* I don't believe that criticism in the realm of human behavior is, in and of itself, constructive. There should be another way to refer to interrupting an unacceptable behavior or practice while offering a replacement. After years of connecting who we are to what we do, it may take many more years of implementing "criticism" differently.

For instance, you can be reasonably certain that when you hear name-calling, you are hearing criticism *Dummy! Lazy bones! Whore! Spoiled brat.* The words themselves are not necessary because a look or an attitude can accomplish the same take-down. "Constructive criticism" is *intended* to motivate a change in behavior. For those of us who've been marinated in shame, criticism does anything *but* motivate our desire to do better.

Another symptom of criticism is the use of global words like *never, ever,* and *always. You never clean your room. Aren't you ever going to get a job? You're always late.* [19]

If the criticism is used with the goal of improving the behavior of the other person, for instance, then undermining confidence by criticising his personhood seldom achieves the improvement desired. Watch a basketball coach angrily yell "Jughead! What's wrong with you?" at the player who misses an easy basket. Does the player's performance improve after that? Suppose a third grader gets three wrong answers on a test and hears, "For crying out loud! I thought you knew better than that." If you were the child, how likely would you be to improve your spelling score? Any motivation to do better might be based solely on avoiding feelings of shame in the future.

What if the coach had said, "Plant your feet before you shoot!" and the parent of the math student had said, "Hmm... not your usual score. Do you want some help getting ready for the next test?"

However, sometimes, when two or more people *have a*

special connection, they might say all manner of what otherwise would be gross and demeaning names to one another. Name-calling in the context of a mutual, respectful relationship can be connecting rather than shaming. You can tell because of the positive responses of those being called names! Dad is smiling when he says, "Rug rats, get in the car!" And the "rug rats" are not hanging their heads or looking humiliated. They're actually liking it! Connection, not separation.

Criticism Covers up Not Knowing

Might criticism be a way for the one criticizing to cover up for not knowing how to name and correct a problem? If the person doing the criticizing can't be clear enough to tell or show the person what to do instead, they are the one who needs to be held accountable. Whatever happened to *I don't know, but I'll find out* or *That's not working. Let's figure out what's going on.*

It's also important to remember that once having been taught a skill, the learner needs to have time and/or times to practice it to gain mastery before they are held fully accountable.

NOW WHAT? Replacing the Be Unclear and Unaccountable Rule

It takes clear boundaries with enforceable consequences to facilitate accountability. In the matter of relationship-building, demonstrating reliability takes doing what we say we will do and being accountable time after time. If the line between what is acceptable and what is unacceptable is drawn well and clearly, each party knows where the other stands. Choices can be made with an eye toward respecting boundaries and in full knowledge of the consequences.

> **NEW RULE 5: Be clear and accountable for your agreements and to your commitments.**

Watching for Language of Responsibility

This discussion about responsible language is based on my own experience. Imagine my surprise when I first learned how much I avoided being responsible! Me, Ms. Responsible!

I had learned to duck being too clear or too responsible unless I was sure I wouldn't be wrong. If I wasn't right, being responsible was like putting a target on my back, so I learned ways to duck, all in an effort to keep others from seeing that I didn't know what (I assumed) I was supposed to know, but didn't.

In the 1980's, I ran into the concept of responsible and irresponsible language,[20] and although I was extremely uncomfortable at first, I began noticing how much I used language that was irresponsible. I also began listening for it in others. I'll mention three of the most common "skirting" techniques involving language.

Saying yes or no straight

I didn't respond to a yes or no question directly. Instead, I beat around the bush, qualifying and softening my answer but without saying a definite yes or no when the question clearly called for a yes or no response.

Now I know that if a friend asks me if I will go for a walk at 10 o'clock, there are any number of responsible ways to answer. *Yes* is one. *No* is another, *Yes or No* with a qualifier or an invitation to negotiate is a third. *Yes, I'd like to walk with you, but are you available to walk at 9 instead of 10?* Compare those to the less responsible and less clear response: *I'm a little tired.* That wasn't answering the question!

When I am the person doing the asking, I now refrain from asking for something to which I am not willing to hear both a Yes or a No response, as in *Will you please set the table now?* If little Billy doesn't have a choice about setting the table, *Billy, please set the table now* is appropriate.

Being clear about who is responsible for what

Oblique, indirect language muddies the water as far as responsibility goes. "The table isn't set." What does *that* mean? My children automatically knew what that meant. Yet I could see how the words themselves, silly and irresponsible as they were, invited a silly and irresponsible answer like *You're right! The table isn't set yet.* Using indirect, unclear language can cause a lot of unnecessary drama and more than enough control battles.

Here is the test for clarity: If the response to a question or request is "So?" it's not clear about who is responsible for what. Meaning is implied, not explicit. I urge you to use the *So?* test in your head. Be aware saying it out loud can be provocative! Try these on for size. *The checking account needs money.* Could your first response be a *So?* In this case, *Did you put money in the checking account today?* is a more direct question. *May I please have a glass of water?* instead of *I'm thirsty.*

An old story makes the point. A hard-to-please passenger thrust her dinner at a flight attendant, saying, "This potato is bad!" Instead of running for a new potato, the flight attendant picked up the potato, shook her finger at it, and admonished the potato directly. "Bad potato. Bad, bad potato."

Although not nearly so much fun to see and tell, the passenger could have said, "This potato is underdone. May I please have another?"

Parents often signal their children that it is time to pick up toys by saying *I need you to pick up your toys.* A clever 3-year-old might disregard the request out of hand. If the obvious response to the request can be *So?* the request is not clear.

Another clever child might hear *I need you to pick up your toys* as an invitation to a power struggle and respond with *I'll do it later.* And adult and child are off to the races. The adult isn't getting what she wants and the child probably is.

In the matter of clarity as to who is responsible for what, how does *Pick up your toys now, please* sound? If the request is followed by *I don't want to,* a good response might be *We'll look forward to seeing you at dinner when you are finished.* This is best said in a calm, firm voice as you exit the room, not waiting for a control battle to ensue.

Redefining from what to where, who to what, and so on to change the topic

In attempting to hold others accountable, another way of slipping from the jaws of responsibility should be noted. It is the skill of not answering the question asked. We're all quite accustomed to its use. So accustomed, we move right on in a conversation as though nothing has happened.

If you've ever tried to hold someone accountable and you end up talking about something quite different from the subject of your concern or question, you have been redefined, redirected, or manipulated, so the other person can avoid being accountable. And it works both ways. You can redefine others as well.

Here's how it works. If you ask someone a WHERE question, listen for a matching WHERE answer. Just so with HOW, WHEN, WHICH, and maybe even WHY quetions. When the answers don't match, the other person is attempting to throw you off your trail of truth-seeking, or has diverted or distracted you from your goal.

Q: WHERE is my credit card?

A: I didn't go to the store today.

If you follow the unmatched response, you wind up not getting your question answered or your problem solved.

Q: HOW did your coat get ripped?

A: I'm not wearing that coat today.

Q: WHEN will your report be done?

A: I'm on page 9 and it needs to be 12 pages.

Q: WHERE is your new red dress?

A: I'm wearing the black one to the dance.

If you ask a question and don't get a matching answer, calmly ask it again...and again...and again. If you try to logically follow the non-matching (and irresponsible) response, you won't get to the point of identifying the problem or solving it. You're more likely to wind up talking about dinner last night, confused and wondering, *How did we get here? What on earth happened back there?* This might also be called "getting the run-around."

If we grew up in a family where it paid to be irresponsible in certain ways, practicing responsible language may feel even more than awkward. We can have a hard time getting it to come out of our mouths. If the world doesn't explode when our language is clear, we may be motivated to try it again. As our confidence grows, after awhile it's mostly automatic. The best outcome is becoming clearer about stating our wants and needs.

Make an assessment of your safety when applying responsible language to your communication repertoire. Don't push for clarity and responsibility with someone who resorts to violence. They are working under their own game rules and looking to be pinned down isn't one of them, not in the way you are thinking of it.

Try implementing responsible language a little bit at a time, starting with the one that represents the lowest risk. At first, when someone asked me a question that required a *yes* or *no* answer, I experienced a small sense of fear. I did it anyway. After stepping out of my comfort zone the first time, it didn't take long for me to risk doing it again. I liked feeling a bit more powerful–in a good way. It's funny how such seemingly small things can make such a big difference.

Confidence comes not from always being right,
but from not fearing to be wrong.

Peter T. McIntyre

Avoiding One Reason for Conflict

Language is a carrier of meaning. And our language can get us in trouble when trouble is not what we're looking for. When words you heard and found unfriendly a long time ago automatically come from your mouth, that's a clue that your attention might be directed toward an old habit. Believe that there *is* a better way to get through to others.

A simple shift in tone can transform a blaming or resentful statement into one that's more likely to be heard. We tend to use blaming as a way to assign responsibility, solve problems, and encourage changes in behavior—and yet blame accomplishes none of these things. An interaction that starts with an accusatory comment tends to end up in a blame-trading marathon that goes nowhere. It goes nowhere, that is, if changing the behavior of someone else is the goal.

Shifting from blaming language to problem-solving language takes some awareness about how angry or disappointed or powerless you feel. After reassuring yourself that an out-and-out blaming might relieve you but doesn't get the problem solved, think about this as a way to express yourself:

First, avoid the accusation and state the facts. Instead of *Why didn't you tell me you'd be late?* try *I was upset when you weren't here at the time we agreed on.* Second, it may be a challenge, but empathize with the offender instead of criticizing. Instead of *At least when I'm late, I call you,* try *I understand what held you up.* And last, make your request for the consideration you seek without a negative tone. Instead of *Just once I wish you weren't so thoughtless about my time,* try *I would feel so relieved if you'd flash me a text when you're going to be late. Will you do that next time?*

All in all, respectful language inspires thoughtful reciprocity in a relationship. You respect me and I respect you. The most delightful benefits are being clear about our needs while, at the same time, deepening trust in treasured relationships.

The truth isn't always beauty, but the hunger for it is.

Nadine Gordimer

Slipping the Hooks, Making the Turn

- Begin monitoring your words for responsible language. If you hear your words as irresponsible, think about how you could say what you said differently and go back and try again, replacing the old words with new ones that make your meaning clearer.
- Begin monitoring the words of others for responsible language. If you are unclear or confused by what someone says, try simply and respectfully asking questions to clarify, as this before and after example illustrates.

Jason's department head asked him to rewrite the copy of a brochure explaining the company's consulting services. Without asking for clarity about the task, Jason delivered the proposed copy to his boss several days later. His boss greeted Jason's work by saying, "I didn't know it would take you so long."

The boss called Jason into his office an hour later. "Is this what you really do? If it is, you've told too much. And the brochure should include the background of the company, And why did you use a question-and-answer format?"

Taken aback, Jason left the boss's office and sorted out what he was feeling and what to do about the boss' reactions. Try again? No, not until he got more clarity first, he decided.

"Jim, I'd like to get a better idea of what the rewrite you want. Yes, the text represents what we really do. Is there a particular format you would suggest? What is the publication department's word limit? How many words should be devoted to the company's background? And what's your deadline for having the revised copy on your desk?"

In this instance, pinning the job down before it was undertaken would have saved time and frustration for all concerned. Practice clarity and practice expecting clarity!

Consider using these guidelines if you are working with someone else's irresponsible language,

- Be assertive about asking for the clarity you need.
- Ask a question again when you don't get a clear reply.
- Say what you say clearly and positively, avoiding accusations and snarkiness.
- Regard promises with respect. Assume if the promise or commitment is sincere, the one making the promise is not simply being placating for the moment. *I promise to stop throwing clothes on the floor and I'll put the dirty ones in the hamper.*

Since a promise needs a consequence for accountability, agreeing to one at the time the promise is made can avoid problems later. *I promise to put my dirty clothes in the hamper and if I don't, you get to assign me a 30-minute job which I agree to complete within 24 hours!* There should also be a lovely consequence, like treating with a favorite meal or simply a warm smile and kiss on the cheek that reinforces compliance! If, for some reason, you find it necessary to remake an agreement, renegotiate the terms considering the age of the other party and nature of the relationship. If chronic failure to comply with agreements, promises, contracts, or commitments is a problem, think about seeing a third party for help. There's something else going on.

- Celebrations for keeping agreements, promises, and the like, are extremely okay!
- Ask yourself how you have avoided setting personal boundaries for your own health and safety by saying "yes" when you may have wanted to say "no." Here are some examples to get you thinking:

    I said "yes"...
    - to be helpful or to be seen as helpful
    - to do what others expected
    - to avoid conflict
    - to rescue by volunteering because others didn't
    - because it was the moral thing to do
    - _____
    - _____

- Read and become familiar with the Structure Chart in Appendix A.

- If you are not totally and perfectly responsible in the coming week, another week will surely follow. Keep your attention on clarifying your boundaries and being persistent. You are becoming an ever more trustworthy and reliable human being.

- For help with New Rule beliefs, see the Affirmations in Appendix B.

Never be afraid to try something new.
Remember, amateurs built the ark.
Professionals built the Titanic.

Author unknown

Moving On

We've been uncovering the shame system rules and how they work together to keep us stuck, or how they invite us to give away our power. In one way or another, each of the seven rules is about accountability or the lack thereof. Looking at the first four rules, it should be more obvious how much they work together to gum up the works leading to Old Rule 5. Nothing seems to be addressed straight-on; everything is crooked. Nothing seems to be secure and predictable; everything is slippery.

Once again, these rules are such an integral part of our cultural fabric, no one is to be blamed for using them as a guide for having relationships, both with ourselves and others. At the same time that few would blame any of us for beginning to replace them with rules that honor the dignity of us human beings.

We now come to uncovering the bottom line rule – the one which all the others conspire to put into effect.

———————

When you arise in the morning, think of what a precious privilege it is to be alive...to breathe, to think, to enjoy, to love.

Marcus Aurelius

———————

CHAPTER NINE

OLD RULE 6: BE IN CONTROL

Manipulate, threaten, coerce, and
use whatever works to get what you need.

Can we afford to surrender to the expression
of the Light we were given?

Ila Benevidez-Heaster

WHAT? The Meaning of the Old Be In Control Rule

For most of us, being out of control is not an attractive option. I'm not even sure what I'd be capable of if I were out of control. Too much has happened in my lifetime not to recognize that other people who are out of control can harm me. We all seem to know we are safest when we're in control of ourselves, but sometimes we can get into real trouble by not acknowledging the limits of our power to control the behavior of others. If *being in control* means to be in control of myself, I think we all have a deep desire for it.

Lily's experience poses an always interesting question about being in control of a situation.

Thirty-something newlywed Lily worked herself silly preparing her first Thanksgiving dinner, which she wanted to be spectacular, for her extended family. And it was. The food was Julia Childs all the way and the table was gorgeously set. Dinner was nearly ready,

Her parents arrived two hours past the time on the invitations. They made no attempt to warn Lily they'd be arriving late. Being late didn't seem to be a problem for them.

But it was a problem for Lily. When her parents didn't show up with the rest of the guests, Lily postponed putting the potatoes on to boil and used whatever means she could to hold dinner. But the turkey was overdone and dry and most of the other food was past its prime. Lily was humiliated and angry, but she said nothing. Armed with that experience, when Lily planned a baby shower for her sister several months later, she solved her problem by inviting her parents two hours earlier than the festivities were set to begin.

Whether arriving late for dinner was the parents' conscious choice or not, it would seem their behavior controlled the situation. Lily's extraordinary dinner was her way of getting the positive attention she craved, which was her way to be in control, but her efforts didn't get her what she wanted. Lily wasn't able to report how her parents felt because she never talked with them about what had happened, never expressed her frustration.

It's not altogether good for human beings to have to go to such great lengths to get what they need. Lily was doing her best to make the perfect dinner. Her parents disrespected Lily and her guests by being unaccountably late, which apparently suited what they needed. You could say there was a control battle going on. Whose needs were being met? Once again both were losers, if we see what's going on from the point of view of an eagle with long sight.

Exploring the Need for Control

Just as the indigenous people of the Far North have many words to describe snow, we must think *control* is a very big deal because we have so many ways to talk about it. Here are some of them:

> *Dominate, rule over, reign over, govern, command, order, dictate. Have it all one's way, call the shots, call the plays, run the show, boss, lay down the law. Hold the purse strings, be in the driver's seat, be in the saddle, wear the pants or the trousers, be in a position of authority, hold all the cards, have well in hand, be master of the situation, be on top of, have under one's thumb.*[21]

It's good to be in control. It's good to be in control of ourselves and our behavior. It's good to be in control of a situation. A life out of control is not attractive or attracting. A speaker stands before an audience and waits for the audience to pay attention, expecting the audience to get quiet and focus on him. That's the moment when each person in the audience chooses to give up control to the speaker, allowing him control of the moment.

It's good to be in control of children or vulnerable adults if *control* means doing for them what they are not capable of doing for themselves, especially in the areas of health, safety, and protection. It is necessary for military forces to be obedient to the commands of the leaders who are charged with being in control. Corporations who knowingly market unsafe products need to be regulated or controlled to protect the buying public. In this and many other ways, control of others is protective and positive.

In circumstances where a leader is over-controlling and those on the receiving end feel disrespected because their needs are not being taken into account, non-compliance or sabotage is a likely response. One rightly asks, "What are the leader's personal needs to be in control?" Where might this need to be in control in relationships originate? There are several possibilities but it has a lot to do with trust.

Where love rules, there is no will to power, and where
power predominates, there love is lacking.
The one is the shadow of the other.

Carl Jung

Going Back to Our Beginnings: The Trust Cycle[22]

Picture a newborn. Babies have no way to get their food or keep their bodies clean and warm or keep themselves safe. They have to do whatever they can to get someone to take care of them. They are powerless to do it themselves, except for one thing. They can cry. So when they're hungry, they cry, and anger quickly gets added to the cry to make it even more demanding. They can go from a whimper to a full roiling boil in a matter of seconds. Getting someone to feed them and meet their needs is a matter of life and death.

Suppose the person who responds to a baby's call for help is so preoccupied with their own needs and problems that there's little or no interest or energy to give the baby what she needs. Or suppose that the baby is hungry and is given a bottle with half-soured milk, and when the baby refuses it, she is yelled at and blamed for being hungry, maybe worse.

Suppose a new dad comes home for lunch and finds his two-week-old baby limp and hoarse from crying to be fed. His wife sits motionless in the chair, eyes empty and frozen with depression. No one intended to be hard on the baby. Nevertheless, if this scene happens over and over again, the baby's primitive and survival-oriented senses, beyond provoking fear, tell her that she lacks the power to get what she needs. Translation: She learns she is not okay and her needs are not okay.

Suppose the baby's cues are read accurately and she is fed and cared for in a responsive, reliable, and nurturing way. That baby is likely to think she's a pretty good signaler. She learns she's effective and can trust that her needs will be met. Translation: She is okay and her needs are okay.

This basic survival behavior in humans isn't all that different from how it works in the animal world.

Babe, the chocolate Lab, lay on a cardboard-covered space on the warm furnace room floor. She was in the midst of a litter of 3-day-old pups. There was plenty of grunting, squeaking, and slurping going on.

Suddenly, a whimper drew the attention of the observers and most of all, Babe. One of the sightless pups had squirmed himself away from his nestlings. His whimper quickly gave way to a terrified distress alarm, a sound that could not be ignored. "I'm way out here! Where are you? I don't know how to get back. I'll die if I don't get back!" His alarm cry intensified.

It didn't take the separated one long to get Babe's attention! She shook the pups off their feeding stations and went to get the errant soul, who was beginning to tire from his all-out effort. Babe seized the pup with a gentle mouth, dropped him into the middle of his mates, and resumed her position. The pup settled himself in the bat of an eye. All was well now.

Yes, the decision to trust, or not to trust, or to what degree to trust, begins early. We might say it's instinctual behavior born of the drive to stay alive.

"Baby" Decisions are Foundational Decisions

NEED...SIGNAL...FULFILLMENT...TRUST. That's the essence of the cycle of learning about control.

The cycle that results in a desperate need to find a way be in control is NEED... SIGNAL... INAPPROPRIATE RESPONSE... MISTRUST. Thus do adaptive kids resort to learning how to manipulate to get what they need to survive.

We're all on a control continuum. Some of us learn to get our needs met by being in control any way that's open to us. Some of us learn to be wary because our care was uneven or inconsistent. And some of us learn to trust in the goodness and competence of others. If we learn that those who care for us are reliable and trustworthy, we come to believe in the goodness and competence in ourselves. However, when things don't go as they should, infants, babies, and children do what they can to develop behaviors that will bring people toward them when they need help. The strategies they develop to take care of themselves are their means of being in control when others are not. Children do whatever works to keep themselves safe and alive.

SO WHAT? Some Effects of the Be in Control Rule

Control and the Family Environment

As children grow, living with the first five shame rules fosters a family climate of uncertainty, suspicion, mistrust, insecurity, and fear–to one degree or another. But family members learn to get along with what they have and where they are. Since human beings go for the best they can get, family members automatically use their will to live and creatively adapt to their circumstances.

In the Williams' family, Millie and Nate figured out that if they took care of their mom's depression and dad's rage episodes, they had a place of effectiveness and belonging in their family.

Millie's way of adapting was to be a good student, a pleasant and placating person, and the pride of her family. Nate, on the other hand, got his attention by being the "bad" kid. Millie would have been mortified if the principal called her out about a problem, while Nate would have reacted with a certain sense of diffident pleasure and relief. Millie's "good" and Nate's "bad" served the same purpose. They both got people to come toward

163

them. They got the recognition they needed. They found ways to get the security they lacked. They found ways to be in control.

Several years ago, I co-taught a parenting class to men in jail. At the start of a set of six classes, not one of the men spoke of his family as anything less than "fine" or "good." One young man even said, "I am lucky to have such good parents." Then one day, when we were talking about how children in a family tend to over-function when a parent under-functions, I saw a tear in that young prisoner's eye and quietly asked, "What are you remembering?"

He said, "While I was at home, I kept my little brother out of the way of my mom's temper when she was drinking. I could take it, but my little brother is getting it all now."

His "I have a great family" picture began getting down to what was more true. Head down and with sadness and remorse, he said quietly, "I can't take care of him when I'm in here."

The prisoner's wish to present himself as having come from a "good" family was his way of protecting himself. Even if the big people abuse and neglect the little ones, the little ones profess their loyalty by protecting the family's facade of goodness, or at the least, their exceptionalism. "We're the best (or baddest) on the block." John Bowlby,[23] the father of attachment theory, has said that no child wishes to acknowledge that his family doesn't love him. Even though he doesn't feel loved by those who are supposed to love him. Better said, no child wishes to acknowledge they are not loved.

Infants and very young children believe they are the centers of the universe. If they don't feel safe and cared for, they take that to mean there is something about themselves that isn't worthy to be taken care of, to be loved. To their developing egocentric brains, their unlovability must be their fault.

We all want families where the small people don't have to take care of the big ones.

No matter what happens, I will handle it...and by admitting I can't handle it, I have handled it.

Unknown

Adapting to the Family Environment

Whenever infants and children are uncertain of the care and protection of their "big people," they find ways to get their human hunger for recognition, structure, and stimulation met. If the adults are under-functioning, the children will over-function, doing their best to keep their People going. The skill of adapting, acquired early in life, grows up to be what is known as *codependence*.

As has been described by many, here are some of the classic ways kids adjust to challenging family conditions:

- Being the kid who is, as a colleague has said, "the family hood ornament," the "good" one who brings credit to the family.
- Being the kid who throws sand in the family gears, not out of meanness but from a desire to get noticed and be connected.

- Being the kid who finds ways to relieve the family's stress with distracting behaviors. "Don't pay attention to (*fill in the blank*). Look over here!"
- Being the "easy" kid; the one doesn't make demands of the family and who neither wants to cause problems nor chase after achievements.

There are many, many variations on these themes. No matter what the adaptation, it serves to stabilize and preserve a child's and the family's existence. It seems the human organism strives for balance because balance means having a measure of predictability.

As a child, Lori adapted to the dynamics in her family by getting sick. She was a classic "good girl," but it was never enough to get basic benevolent, unearned attention from her father. As an adolescent, she played the piano for church services and the congregation appreciated and admired her skill, but her father took the credit as his. After all, he paid for the lessons. She learned that playing the piano to shine the light on him and the family secured her belonging. However, as a child she also learned that getting sick resulted in getting attention that was hers alone. When she got sick, she got nurtured.

Years later, Lori's husband would call their married daughter, Ashley, whenever Lori had a health episode. Ashley knew the call was her summons to get to her mother's side. Ashley said she would rather have her mother call ahead of the episode and say, "I miss you. Will you come for a cup of coffee and a visit?" if that's what she really wanted.

Instead, getting summoned to relieve her mother's loneliness created more feelings of resentment and separation in Ashley than feelings of connection. "It was hard to have a relationship with Mother. She talked a lot about her health, but I knew there was more to her. Her health wasn't all of who she was. I'm sad that I was never able to get past what felt like a huge barrier and get to know her better."

The variations of adaptations to get needs met in uncertain family environments can become so relied upon and ingrained they come to be referred to as addictions. At the very least, our adaptations become part of our identity or our identity confusion. *I am a helper. I am a problem. I don't know who I am.*

Feeling like we're in control of a person, place, or thing can, at least temporarily, relieve emotional pain or distress. Paradoxically, the control we gain initially almost inevitably evolves into a lack of control, which is where we started. Our getting-in-control adaptation to our powerlessness often becomes another powerless situation. Alcohol and other drugs, shopping, gambling, work, religion, image, illness, eating disorders, hoarding, the acquisition of money, exercise, status, or striving for control of another person. Just about anything is fair game.

Too often, the addiction becomes the relationship of first choice and those who want a relationship with the *real* person will be disappointed, They will try and try forever and/or go away empty. No person or family sets out to have it this way. Hope, on the other hand, lies in shedding unwanted behaviors we developed for good reason and moving toward more New Rule life-affirming options.

Love is the condition in which the happiness of
another person is essential to your own.

Robert Heinlein

Controlling Others

Let's begin with this: Without the use of force, an adult has no ordinary means beyond natural and logical consequences to get another person to do what that person doesn't want to do. That doesn't mean we don't try.

The old family rule of Be and Do Right necessitates being in control of how the family looks to the larger community: the neighborhood, the church, the social set, colleagues, competitors, and so on. In leadership situations, people tend to reach back into their own experience at the hands of leaders, the style they experienced in their families of origin. A couple of reference points about family leadership can help us here.

Researcher and author Diana Baumrind[24] identified four styles of family leadership. One is **authoritative**, where the leader is seen as having knowledge and experience and expects others to share responsibility for functioning. They expect their children to function within family structures and are responsive to their needs. Studies show that children reared in families with authoritative leadership develop a good sense of themselves, are more confident, and are better equipped to conduct their own lives.

Another style is **authoritarian**, where the leader dictates how members are to function, usually without much input from the members. Children reared under authoritarian leadership are not encouraged to do their own thinking or to challenge family leadership. The leaders do the thinking and the members are expected to do what the leader says.

The third parenting style is **permissive**, where leaders have a low value on structure, have either too much or too little nurture, and have few expectations of members.

Uninvolved is a fourth parenting style which names a style of meeting children's most *basic* needs but with little attention paid to interacting with them.

The authoritarian "my way or the highway" approach is familiar to families where control is an issue for the leader(s). An authoritarian leader tends to dominate. Discussion, when it occurs, ends with a winner and a loser, and every thought or opinion is labeled *good* or *bad*. If the leader sees her job as getting others to do what *she* wants or needs, she will manipulate others with whatever it takes when requests, edicts, or mandates don't work.

A proper negotiation involves each party presenting information relative to the problem, followed by discussion. This is how children learn how to think (evaluate, identify options, project outcomes, etc.) and to make balanced decisions.

Authoritarian leaders make decisions without involving or valuing the input of, or the impact on, the group's constituents (family members). By disregarding or even disparaging the thinking or feelings of members, the leader communicates *Don't be* and *Don't think* messages to those he is supposed to be nurturing and protecting. Many rigid authoritarians *intend* to be loving and protective, but their style doesn't fully convey this to those "under" them.

Mary's parents sound a lot like authoritative parents. It

would seem they pictured their children and themselves as loving, competent. and growing.

Mary said, "I loved dinnertime when I was growing up. The food was good but the conversations were better. Dad believed that children should learn to think and he and Mom were masters at encouraging my brother and me to observe, question, and identify alternatives. That's probably why my brother is a successful attorney and I've had a long career in public health. I rely on my critical thinking. I don't challenge an idea just for the sake of challenging. I challenge to understand issues and opinions and facts. I'm forever grateful to my folks because I can see how I've passed that skill down to my kids!"

The Nurture and Structure charts in Appendix A contain further information on the effects of parenting styles. The Nurture Chart has six positions from which we can nurture children (and ourselves); the center two positions are helpful in strengthening Authoritative parenting; the other four positions signal less than helpful, or even hurtful, ways of nurturing. The same is true for the Structure Chart. Remember, the two center positions are the strongest.*

---

* The reader may think of the Nurture and Structure Charts as a Highway. The center two positions are like a solid road, safest and most secure. Working outward, the next two positions are like the soft and unreliable shoulders of the highway, troublesome and a warning to find out how to get back onto the firm road. The outside positions are like ditches and often require a towtruck to get us out and into position to drive in the center lanes.

You say you do, but how could you possibly know what's
good for me? You are not the expert of me. I am.

Anonymous

The Delusion of Being in Control of Others

It is important to be realistic about what is within your control and what lies beyond your control. An experience I had long ago always leaps to mind when I think about believing I am in control.

On the back end of the acreage on which my family lived when I was 10 was a sand pit. Our grassy pasture ended abruptly and each year, the edge of the pit grew slowly toward our house. As I looked up from the road that ran along the bottom, the pit looked very high.

We kids would play a game of Who Could Crawl Up the Highest. If I scrambled as carefully and gently as I could up the face of the pit, I made some momentary headway but I'd always slip back with the sand as it gave way and rippled to the bottom, taking me with it. The more effort I put into scrambling, the more I slipped back. We were crazy to think we could actually get all the way to the top.

We got a dose of reality the day we heard faint screams of "Help! Help me!" Racing across the pasture to the top of the sand pit, we looked down to see a man frantically digging with his hands at a pile of sand at the foot of the pit. "My son!" he screamed. Dad flew down the hill and joined the man in digging furiously. By the time the alarm had sounded and others had come to help, it was too late.

Whenever I think of trying hard to be in control, I think of scrambling up that steep slope of sand. The harder I scramble to be in control, the more out of control I feel. Plus the sand can bury me.

None of us can control anyone other than ourselves, much as we'd like to. As adults, we make choices for ourselves. We decide to either duck or accept the consequences. In the same way, we presume that others are also entitled to make choices for themselves. We're on firmer ground when we mind our business and expect others to mind theirs.

In what might be an apocryphal story, Gandhi was asked how, in colonial days, so relatively few British soldiers could control the vast population of India. He is said to have replied, "They humiliate us to control us."

The Old Rules necessarily result in a lot of humiliation for the sake of being in control. The New Rules are meant to underscore our dignity as human beings.

Shaming Strategies Used to Have Control of Others

In surveying the landscape of control, the strategies of manipulation are many, varied, and familiar. They are found whenever the old rules are in force and they are based on shame and shaming — exposing what isn't "right" about the person so they can more easily be controlled. Here are some of the most common:

- *What on earth is wrong with you? Why are you a kid I can never count on?* Instead of pointing out faults, calling names, and criticizing, try reporting behaviors accurately and telling or showing the person a way to improve. *You're a sharp kid. I'll show you how to do that job. If you have a problem you need help with, ask me and we'll figure it out together.*

- *I don't have time to listen to any of your stories and stop moping around the house.* Instead of ignoring, disregarding, or shunning, listen compassionately to what is being said or felt, intending to understand what the other person needs. *Let's go out for a walk. I want some time to catch up with you.*

- *You don't have (use) the brains you were born with!* Instead of using words that humiliate and ridicule, try *I respect you for trying so hard. Do you want help finding another way that might work out better?* or *Here, try it this way and let me know how it works.*

- *You're 19 and as long as you live under my roof and eat my food, you'll do things my way or feel free to leave!* The New Rule way would have the parent remaining constant and connected while working through differences instead of abandoning or threatening to abandon the other. *Unless you're going to school, I think it's time for you to either do chores and pay some rent here or begin looking for a way to be out on your own.*

Or *Look, this arrangement isn't working out for me. I'm resenting you and I definitely do NOT want to resent you. Are you willing to stick together and hassle this through until we find something that works better for both of us?*

And if that invitation is declined, try *I love you and wish the best for you, but it's not good for me to go on like this. I'd like us to see a counselor, meaning a neutral party. Will you go with me?*

And if that option is brushed aside, try *I love you. You're welcome to stay here for another four weeks, by which time you will have found another place to live.*

There are some methods of control that aren't always seen as such. These behaviors originate as adaptations to uneven conditions in the Old Rule family and are problematic when they become patterns of behavior that are relied upon for structure, stimulation and security. Here are some examples:

- Attracting or repelling others by being overly charming, unpredictable, helpless: angry or rageful.
- Being domineering and not taking the other into account.
- Establishing intellectual, social, and moral superiority instead of seeing all parties as individuals who are learning and growing in their own right.
- Teasing unmercifully by making a "joke" at the other's expense, when it's obvious the other person is not enjoying it.
- Being overly solicitous in taking care of another's expressed or unexpressed needs in hopes the receiver of their largesse will see also see the giver's needs and meet them.
- Creating an illusion of infallibility or grandiosity instead of being humble and honest about their competencies.
- Public personal attacks, whether true or not.

An automatic reaction of wanting to hide or strike out can be a reliable way of knowing when another's controlling behaviors are directed toward us. Our on-board warning system says: *Stop. Think. What's going on here?* So we stop and say something like: "I'll think about what you've said (done) and get back to you."

The *thinking* part goes back to two questions:

Who's responsible for what?

Whose needs are being served?

The Need to Win Control Battles

Conflicts are inevitable in this life: conflicts of needs, conflicts of beliefs, conflicts of values, and conflicts of goals. Shame-based rules lay out a battleground rife with invitations to engage in control battles. Where mistakes are unacceptable, winning will "prove" rightness, making winning particularly important. When two parties have a difference of opinion, it isn't especially pretty when both have so much at stake.

Disagreements are part of life. Disagreements don't have to signal the need for a war. Wars are desperate measures taken when winning is the only option. Wars are less likely between people of good will who sit around the problem-solving table, their good intentions outranking any wish to win or protect themselves from "losing."

No one needs to know everything. No one needs to be right all the time. What an interesting idea!

The Fear of Being Out of Control

The fear of being out of control often provokes upping the means and methods of being *in* control.

Robert, the dad of 13-year-old Darius, doesn't want him

walking to school with his friend, Ashley Ann. Robert has never told Darius why he is so concerned, and Darius doesn't understand why his dad is so unreasonable. The truth is, when Robert was 16, he had sex with his girlfriend. As he says, "I let my body outrun my commitment to use birth control."

Seldom, do people seek to have an "I lost control" sign hung around their necks or look for a chance to be exposed as a person of uncertain character.

Consider the unplanned pregnancy of an unmarried woman. In cultures and communities where this is contrary to community or religious rules, the pregnancy is a problem, not only for the pregnant one and the baby, but for her family. *What will they think of us?* The pregnancy itself can be evidence of the family's failure to be in control of their daughter's behavior.

Long ago, in cultures such as ours, pregnant unmarried women and girls were sent away to have their babies, relinquish those babies for adoption, and then return home saying they'd been "visiting an aunt in a distant city." In effect, the baby was exiled to protect the mother and her family from the judgments of a community that believed extramarital sex was shameful. The infant was given a new birth certificate replacing the birthparents' names with the names of the adopting parents. The files containing the original birth certificates were legally sealed away. Thus, any proof of failure to control sexual urges was kept secret, secret for the birth mother and her family and secret for the often unnamed lover.

There are innumerable examples of loss of control. Commiting a crime, gambling away a fortune, beating your children, failing to prevent another from commiting suicide, cruelty to animals. The list is long.

The need to keep incidents of losing control a secret is

understandable. We're sensitive to keeping our so-called failures from exposing a shameful inadequacy. "Why?" you may ask. Because the fear of exposure of our inadequate selves carries an implied punishment like shunning, loss of status, demeaning, or being cast out. No wonder we have a self-protective motivation to avoid others knowing when we've slipped up.

And as we let our own light shine, we unconsciously
give other people permission to do the same.
As we are liberated from our own fear, our
presence automatically liberates others.

Nelson Mandela

Every Battle for Superiority Has Two Losers[25]

Control battles are most often fought over a conflict of needs and desires. *I want to get a dog and you don't. I want our child to attend public school and you want her to attend private school.* These kinds of differences can be managed with good problem-solving techniques which include gathering relevant data, sorting through options, and projecting outcomes. Even before that, both parties must be clear about their beliefs and values. A third and impartial party can serve as an objective voice helping the parties to clarify their goals and their process.

However, when two or more people have an iron in the fire and one *has* to prevail over the other(s), that means a battle for control. *Pick up your toys. I'm not done playing with them.* And so on. *Hang up your clothes. I don't mind the wrinkles.* And so on. It's best to carefully pick the control battles you get into because in parenting, once you get into one, you probably should win it, since your job is to win the ones that keep children safe. *You will not drive the car alone until its legal to do so and I'm satisfied you'll drive responsibly.*

In an Old Rules family, controlling others has special meaning. Winning and losing involves being and doing right, but only the controller's way. If a person with an authoritarian frame of reference "gets one over" on others, he proves his superiority to himself. If he is successful in establishing his superior authority, his hope is that no one will see how flawed he really believes or fears himself to be. At some deeper level, he's scared he'll lose it all.

How might that win be achieved? By issuing an order. Then by escalating the intensity of the demands. There might be coercion concerning money or privileges. There are humiliations and threats. If all else fails to gain control, in a final attempt to prevail, force is used. This dynamic is played out in the home, in bureaucracies and the workplace, and among nations. And notice, whether the controller wins or loses, the problem that supposedly started the control battle remains unresolved or postponed. If the goal is to have an even and honorable relationship, shaming to control for superiority is not the way to get it. By taking an opponent down, the superior one goes down too, in the end.

According to a recent study,[26] "People in power are able to lie better." Dana Carney, Ph.D., one of the study's authors, went on to say, "It just doesn't hurt them as much to do it." And "...power acted as a buffer allowing the powerful to lie significantly more easily. Only low-power individuals felt bad after lying." Carney said the research doesn't show that power leads to lying, but it does suggest dishonesty comes easier to those in power.

The fear of being punished for not knowing the answer is
an important part of every authoritarian mindset of control
because it uses shame, blame, criticism, ridicule, threat
and punishment to intimidate, thus making it frightening
to even question the deeper spiritual truths of life.

Mano Warren

NEW RULE 6: Ask for what you need.
Be willing to negotiate. Be responsible
for yourself and to others.

NOW WHAT? Replacing the Be in Control Rule

No family is perfect, but they're meant to be as trustworthy and reliable as they can be–where kids don't have to manipulate to get connected and be protected. We all crave a place to belong, a place we are safe, or as Christopher Lasch puts it, families are meant to be a "haven in a heartless world.[27] That's a good thought and we just haven't known what's held us back from making it a greater reality.

Shame Hooks Revisited

An early and erroneous belief in our diminished worth increases susceptibility to subsequent shame hooks throughout our lives. Words or deeds occurring in current time connect back to the original shame we experienced and can elicit the same worthlessness or not-good-enough feelings we felt then.

Lynne went to a fine clothing store, telling the helpful clerk she had to have a new outfit for an upcoming special event. The clerk asked, "What kind of thing are you looking for? Any particular style or color?"

Lynne shook her head and shrugged her shoulders. The clerk took over. "You have a sort of Columbo look."

"What does she mean?" thought Lynne. She didn't ask.

The clerk continued. "Casual, on the slouchy side, nothing that stands out." And she went off to assemble an outfit Lynne might look good in. Lynne tried it on and when she looked in the mirror, she drew herself up, surprised by what she saw. She looked fabulous! The clerk had caught a style, colors, and a fit that suited Lynne to a tee. Then she began losing her momentary sparkle. "I'm not sure. I'll have to think about it," she told the clerk.

A few years later a support group member asked her why she didn't buy the outfit. "A little bit of me felt I was misrepresenting who I was, but I think the big reason was that I just didn't want to call that much attention to myself. I'll have to think about where that came from."

Strong early beliefs in our level of security and enoughness is an inoculation from being taken down by individuals and situations where we might otherwise feel shamed, even inadvertently.

A shame-aware friend recently declared, "I think this guy at work is the first person I've met that doesn't have a speck of shame."

"How can you tell?"

"Because he doesn't take any conflict or failure personally. And he doesn't look for a fault, either his or someone else's, when a problem comes up. It's like he has a filter on criticism. I want one of those because he seems so comfortable with himself. He doesn't get pissy when there's a problem. He just seems to have an attitude of 'Oh, well. Let's see what this is about.' He's very easy to be around."

It's common for the echoes of prior shaming to surprise us. Call it shame PTSD. Shame gets attached to a shaming event in our past. We're not thin enough, smart enough, active enough, creative enough, tall enough. There's the shame of being born with learning difficulties, a certain skin color, national origin, or sexual orientation. Shame about a mental health diagnosis, or being in poverty in spite of being a hard worker, or living on the wrong side of the tracks. The shame of being or having been, sexually and/or physically abused. The shame visited upon us by bullies who were themselves steeped in shame. The residual shame of having been actively or passively humiliated by parents. A shaming experience gets triggered in many ways. We're all vulnerable to being hooked by events and people today that are attached to the shaming events and people of yesterday.

There are some things we can do to deal with shame PTSD. Revisiting a shame history can be daunting, but facing down prior shaming and see it as going back and belonging to whomever or whatever originated it can be part of freeing ourselves from shame's bind.

A first step is to recognize the clues to when we may be

under the influence of old shame in present time. Here are some of them:

- Feeling anger and resentment, even rage
- Feeling confused
- Feeling shut down or held back
- Withdrawing
- Having to explain yourself and being defensive
- Comparing yourself to others and being on the short side of the comparison
- Experiencing depression, low energy, feelings of being "stuck"
- Feeling isolated, alone; isolating yourself
- Feeling powerless, hopeless
- Walking on eggshells, afraid of saying or doing the "wrong" thing

Second, connect your current shame trigger with past occurrences to discover the point of origin. What incident, comment, criticism, discounting, abandonment, name-calling, or whatever triggered the current feelings of shame? Now, re-think and re-feel. Re-think the point of origin to look for the kernel of truth that *might* be there. Re-feeling the points of origin is part of this process to put shame in its place. Consider getting the help of a therapist or counselor.

Don't keep what's not yours. If you've learned what you can from this old shame, visualize it flowing back to the person(s) or situation where the shame feelings occurred. If you experienced an attack or surprise hit, chances are pretty good that the other person may have been off-loading their shame onto you.

In a perfect world, none of the shame-connected events beyond our control would have existed in the first place! Whatever the source of shame, any number of triggers can send us right back into feeling small and powerless in real time. Many of the shame-originating situations we experienced when we were young were connected to what was going on with the person doing the shaming. Tragically, their words and actions toward us were more about them than they were about us. That is why changing how we treat ourselves and others is so important. One more thing: We had no control over being born into poverty, of having a schizophrenic mother, or being born gay, or being abused. We *do* have control about how we handle our stories and what we pass on to others.

If people wanted you to write warmly about
them, they should've behaved better.

Anne Lamott

When You've Had a Shame "Hit"

Being hooked, having our buttons pushed, experiencing a trigger that brings up feelings about former experiences will happen in the most surprising ways and at unexpected times. When we feel the "sharp stick in the heart" moment, we can plan a response, or two or three, ahead of time.

- "I'd like to think about that. I'll get back to you when I'm ready."

- "It's clear we don't agree."
- "Would you be more specific? I'm uncertain about what you're saying."
- "Will you say that in a different way?"
- "That's not something I choose to argue about."
- (Looking puzzled and confused.) "Give me a moment to digest what you've just said."

Ergo, in our confusion, we may strike back. The controller counts on the fact that ambushing will work in his favor by catching us off-guard. However you respond, keep these things in mind:

- Take time to evaluate what was said or done. Our shame voices tend to say, "See! I knew you weren't perfect" and we might tend to agree too quickly. Stop. Look for the kernel of truth that may lie hidden in the situation. If you find one that is yours, accept responsibility for only that part and resist the urge to insist that the other is the "bad guy."
- Reflect on the situation. If you see a pattern of control in the relationship in question, ask yourself if the relationship is one that's good for you. If it isn't, plan an exit.

Perhaps our greatest power lies in the security of being seen and being okay with the person we know ourselves to be. When we make mistakes, we fix them. As far as hooking shame goes, you can't reel me in if I don't bite. You can't get me if there's nothing to get gotten.

Being Bullied

Bullying should properly be called "shaming," for the bully goes after a *supposed* defect in another's personhood. He then uses humiliation to heap contempt on his target. In certain psychological circles, this is *projective identification* at work; the bully goes after others for a desire or behavior he, himself, harbors or is guilty of doing. Bullying broadcasts more about the bully than about the bullied. The bully may be treating others the way she was treated. She literally may not, in the words of a 3-year old, "know no better."

If the bully has a problem with the bullied, hurting others is *not* a way to address it. Understanding that the bully has a reason behind her bullying doesn't make it okay. Stopping bullying serves to point out that shaming others is unacceptable.

Bullying comes in many forms. Direct person-on-person bullying. Advertisements that shame in order to sell a product. Like *What's wrong with you; you are out of step.* Or pointing out a so-called mistake in how we're dressed means we are a person unworthy of positive regard. An overly aggressive sales person or suitor who implies they know more about what we want and need than we do, uses shame to get what he needs. True, this isn't as overt as actual taunting and name-calling and other demeaning words and gestures. But the purpose is to manipulate in order to get a pay-off for themselves. Our benefit is not on their radar!

In a culture where shame and shaming are the norm rather than the exception, we may have kept our distance when we witnessed someone being bullied. Who wants to step into the line of fire when the expectation is that we will be included in the bully's assault? Yet, the more we duck a bystander's opportunity to stand up *against* that assault, the more we passively encourage it. That doesn't mean taking up the cudgel against the bully. It doesn't mean joining the fight to make somebody wrong. It means calmly stepping up to focus our attention on the safety of the bullied. Not only physical safety, but emotional safety too. The actions of a bystander who sees to the welfare of the one being bullied gives a powerful message about the inhumanity of shaming.

Stay aware of bullying in all its forms. None of us deserves being bullied and remarkably, when we carry our Light with confidence, the ones who would bully seem to sense our message. We can make ourselves vulnerable to being loved and invulnerable to being preyed upon all at the same time.

Dealing with Disparate Needs Productively

People of good faith who don't need to win all the time can disagree and, in the process, become closer because they understand one another better. The following tips characterize interactions that have a better than even chance of helping us get to a good outcome:

- Decide to come to the metaphorical table with a Do It Well (not Do It Right) rule.
- Listen with compassion to learn the meaning or impact of a troublesome situation.
- Decide not to respond merely by leaping in to defend yourself.
- Practice vulnerability.
- Be willing to say *I may be wrong.*

- Use responsible and respectful words.
- Be willing to negotiate to find a middle ground.
- Look at the other during the discussion.
- Don't agree just to be pleasing. Your needs are important.
- Smile once in a while.

Much has been written about conflict resolution. An Internet search will unearth plentiful resources in the areas of conflict resolution and communication that are beyond the scope of this book. Know that those with deeply internalized shame may feel blocked from working through and mutually resolving conflicts. Find what will work for you.

Slipping the Hooks, Making the Turn

I've never forgotten what a former colleague said years ago. He thought that control was the bottom line issue in any human life. After watching my life and the lives of friends and clients, I have to agree. These activities can help you begin to get more acquainted with the role that control plays in *your* life:

- Keep a lookout for the ways control shows itself in your life and the lives of others.
- Practice dealing with disagreements using the model suggested in this chapter. Listen to others. Listen to yourself. Resist the urge to be defensive. Be clear about what you need. Use respectful and responsible words. Negotiate to find common ground. Review what went well and what you would like to do differently the next time. Try again.

- Review the features of authoritarian and authoritative leadership in the Controlling Others section of this chapter. Which word is more likely to describe someone leading using the New Rules?

- What kind of leader do you prefer when you are the follower?

- Delve into your own experience. What could anyone say or do to control you? What can others say or do that hooks you into frozenness or rage or perfectionism? What words, behaviors, and situations tend to leave you feeling humiliated and/or powerless? Think about where these shame buttons originated. If someone passed shame on to you, let it flow back to them and see yourself as whole. Give back to them what is not yours. You can visualize the shame as an object that's been hurled at your midsection; visualize handing it back to the one off-loading their shame on you.

- Think about your personal shame-originating situations. Write down what you know about the important players in a couple of scenarios. Do you find anything in their history that accounts for *that* person's shame experience? Abandonment, rigidity, perfectionism, physical and/or emotional abuse, neglect? Practice compassion.

- Practice asking for what you need from a person likely to be receptive. If another person asks for something from you that doesn't fit with what would be good for you, politely decline. Agreeing to something and then resenting the other person is being hard on yourself and the other person, too. In those situations where you decide to agree in spite of your reluctance, do so with a full heart. Let go of expectations. Monitor your feelings.

- Refer to the affirmations in Appendix B. Use them to replace old voices with ones that speak more to the truth of who you are.
- One way to deal with shame is to come out of hiding. The fellow who makes a mistake, announces it as a mistake, and immediately takes steps to correct it, doesn't have to go through the endless stressful dance of pretending, avoiding, and protecting himself.
- Pat yourself on the back for your courage to try out new beliefs and behaviors.
- Take your time. Resist the urge to make changes abruptly. Let everything unfold in its own time.

The friendships which last are those wherein each friend respects the other's dignity to the point of not really wanting anything from him.

Cyril Connolly

Moving On

The system of shame-based rules is almost complete. Each rule plays its own particular part. This much is clear. The system as a whole has a way of twisting our knickers to keep us stuck. It is the shroud that limits our Light.

It's possible we can't change it. It stands to reason that if the shroud is still over our eyes and consciousness, it's supposed to be there. But that's hard to believe. That's like being in jail without the key.

The last rule, Deny Reality, stands as a guard protecting the other six.

Sometimes it's a form of love just to talk to somebody that you have nothing in common with and still be fascinated by their presence.

David Byrne

CHAPTER TEN

OLD RULE 7: DENY REALITY

What's going on is not really going on.
Acccept discrepant behaviors and occurrences as normal.

And so, we come to the last rule. The family that bases its interactions on the Old Rules is likely to be confused about reality. No wonder wires are crossed and reality gets all knotted up. Schooled in rules 1 through 6, it's hard to see how it could be otherwise.

- Rule 1. Don't make mistakes.
- Rule 2. Blame someone or something else for your mistakes and shortcomings.
- Rule 3. Don't acknowledge your feelings.
- Rule 4. Don't tell the truth. Keep secrets.
- Rule 5. Don't expect people to be accountable.
- Rule 6. Be in control in all your interactions.

Remember, the rules are not stated as such; they're not posted or negotiated. Their existence is denied. Those to whom the rules apply must navigate their way by the implicit rules as they understand them, for the rules don't exist! That's hard core denial.

Reality is the number one cause of insanity among those who are still in contact with it.

Unknown

WHAT? The Meaning of the Old Deny Reality Rule

Why Denial?

Denial keeps a lid on reality when reality means being exposed for misdeeds, mistakes, and shortcomings. Among many possible answers to Why Denial? are the following:

- Wishing to avoid emotional pain
- Needing to avoid rocking the boat
- Lacking power in a situation (child)
- Believing we have no power in a situation (adult)
- Maintaining an image of ourself or our family
- Believing there are no solutions to the problem
- Being afraid for our safety
- When solving one problem might reveal or lead to even more or greater problems
- Fearing changing whatever is known and predictable

Being in a state of denial keeps us from solving problems. Some problems are easily solved. The parties involved get around the table, put the problem in the middle, and apply their expertise to put an agreed-upon solution in place. However, a point of disagreement or a bone of contention among the members constitutes a problem in itself. Here's where people being honest about their vested interests becomes important.

Imagine a family around the table. The problem: Becky, 16, is stealing from family members and was suspended from school for being intoxicated on campus. Dad and Mom drink daily and Mom's been pulled over for driving while under the influence. If Mom and Dad have a *relationship* with their drug of choice, they run the risk of having to change their use if they acknowledge Becky's problems, so they don't. *Becky's been really stressed at school. Becky's friends are no good. I did this when I was a teenager and I turned out okay. We don't need any help; we'll handle it. This will blow over.*

Problem solving requires at least three things:

- agreement as to what constitutes the problem
- accurate information relative to the problem
- acknowledging the needs and intentions of the persons charged with solving it

If the problem belongs to you and you alone, solve it. If the problem involves someone else, that someone else has to see the same problem you do, *and* be willing to address it. Past denials can stand like a boulder on the path to solutions.

At any level, high or low, in whatever shape you are in, you are the most beautiful creation, you are. I was astonished to find that there was no evil in any soul. I said, "How can this be?" The answer was that no soul was inherently evil. The terrible things that happened to people might make them do evil things, but their souls were not evil. What all people seek, what sustains them, is love, the Light told me. What distorts people is a lack of love.

Mellen-Thomas Benedict[28]

Denial as a Way of Life

It's an insult to know that what you believe is true and have that truth held in disregard, even in contempt. Some people are so good at twisting reality that we're easily made to feel crazy.

"You have my blue pen."

"What blue pen?"

"The one in your hand."

"This pen is mine."

"No, it isn't. I saw you take it from my desk."

"There you go again! I didn't take it from your desk. What's wrong with you?"

That's called crazy-making for good reason. However, most shame-based families are in *unconscious denial*. They don't set out to be in denial to keep from solving problems. Even so, to one degree or another, it's where a lot of families wind up.

Here's how it can work. When a new problem surfaces, the Old Rules family faces it with a certain slipperiness that avoids addressing it. Smooth it over. Park it. Ignore it. Cover it up. The problem simply goes on. If the problem escalates, so does the denial.

If young Johnny should ask an innocent question about *the problem*, he is likely to be summarily shut down, and the content of his question neutralized. Each new problem that crops up has a long line of previously denied and unsolved problems behind it, like a car dragging a long string of rattling tin cans the car's occupants quite honestly don't hear.

Old Rules practitioners don't realize that their growth and maturation has been, and is being, stunted or stopped. But denial has a way of shutting a system down. Often, the family, or the company or community or even a nation, is burdened by a build-up of unresolved problems or issues left for them by previous generations. Few would choose to pass on such an unwanted and limiting legacy, but if they remain unconscious to historical patterns, they are doomed to repeat them.

Across the board, denial is the surest sign that growth is being arrested and a violation of the human spirit is taking place. Any organism, plant or animal, that isn't busy growing, is busy dying. The same is true of any family. The very definition of *growth* implies the ability to move into new territory or situations in a dignifying way and addressing the problems or circumstances encountered there.

It's Not a Problem If It Doesn't Exist

In situations where the powers that be are determined to maintain the status quo, facts are irrelevant. By anyone's definition, George's dad was the lord and master of his household. He claimed his reality and did everything he could to enforce that reality on his wife and kids, seemingly to prove his unassailable power over them.

George's dad went to great lengths to be in control of his children. To that end, George and his three siblings were humiliated time and time again. His brother and two sisters fell in line; George was the one who wouldn't cave in to his dad's too-familiar ridiculous demands.

One day, Mom was making dinner and George was peeling potatoes. Dad wandered in, and for his own reasons, demanded that George say, "I think you, Dad, are the smartest, best dad in the world." George refused to say what he didn't believe! His dad picked up a large onion from the counter and directed his son to sit down at the table. George sat down. So did his dad.

"Eat the onion," Dad said, plopping it down before his son.

"Eat the onion? You mean take a bite of it?"

"I said, 'Eat the onion.' That means eat the onion."

George declined and held out as long as he could, but in light of Dad's powerful and escalating insistence, George knew the next step was not going to be pretty. Not for him. Not for his brother and sisters. Not for his mom.

George took a small bite of the onion, grimaced, shuddered, and put it down on the table. "Didn't I say to eat the whole thing unless you tell me I'm the smartest dad in the world?" said Dad.

George held his ground but Dad made him sit there, mocking and ridiculing George the whole time. It took hours. George's retching and gagging had no effect on Dad's resolve. George felt absolutely powerless to do anything but eat the entire onion, as his dad demanded.

To this day, George's siblings and his mother, who had all witnessed the event, deny it ever happened.

After George told this story, he said, "My family was so crazy, I used to pray I was adopted and hoped someone would come and rescue me. At some point, I gave that up and resolved to get out of there as soon as I could. Meanwhile, to survive, I spent as much time as possible anywhere but at home."

Pretending and Avoiding

If we're not in George's position, from a distance, it's probably easy to see what's happening. If we *are* in his position, and his mother and sibs have been trained not to acknowledge what's really going on, what then? Who does George believe, himself or his family? No wonder many of us have a hard time telling reality and fantasy apart.

Reality is what is real. It's actuality. It's documentable. Our picture of reality should be able to be confirmed by others who see or experience reality the same way. Therein lies the rub. Every person in the same situation may have a different description of what happened because we all experience, observe, and remember through our own unique windows. We all bring past and present experiences and biases to our witnessing.

We can argue about reality, but one thing is undeniable. What's happening is real for the person experiencing it and should never be ridiculed or dismissed. It must be heard and checked out. In mental health circles, to say someone is in touch with reality is a positive statement. To say someone is out of touch with reality is quite another thing, for it suggests distortions of reality or incongruent realities are present. When realities match or match closely, we have confidence that what we hear or see is as close to *true* as we can get.

Do family members *like* living in a swirl of never-being-sure-what-is-real unpredictability? It's not a matter of liking it. It's a matter of coping with what is familiar and supported in the family until the stress becomes too much to handle and the problem(s) can no longer be denied. This can be said about adults. Children have far fewer options. They are literally the prisoners of denial.[29]

SO WHAT? Some Effects of the Deny Reality Rule

Coming Out of Denial

It's no small matter, making a change. The very definition of *risk* is taking a stand or action and not being able to predict or be certain of the outcome. Changing means leaving the familiar behind in favor of the unfamiliar.

To avoid making a change is a deep reason for not facing reality. For instance, if we grow up developing the adaptive *identity* of Caregiver and Helper, that's our reason for belonging, for being accepted by a person or group. Being in a Caregiving and Helping position can also give us a way of feeling effective. Of having a purpose. If we're not being Caregiver and Helper, who are we? Furthermore, if we stop, where and how will we belong?

If we face what we're denying, what happens to our relationships, constructed on what may turn out to be a fabrication of ourselves? We have to really *want* change, or get pushed to the limits of our pain tolerance to actually do it.

Allison was in what she eventually would call a dead marriage. She calls it that in retrospect because she didn't acknowledge it at the time. What she now calls lame attempts to build more positive connections with her husband hadn't worked, much to her dismay.

When she married, she more or less gave up what identity she had and allowed it to flow right into her husband's. Brad said this...Brad thinks that.... Allison functioned in her marriage by doing what she thought would make Brad happy. But Brad did not reciprocate. Caretaking was Allison's way of loving, but Brad did not return her "love" in kind. Over the years, giving so much and getting little in return resulted in growing resentment. She feared confronting any problems beneath the resentment. The idea of being on her own never even entered her mind.

She secretly prayed Brad would have an affair or drink away his paycheck because those would be good-enough excuses to leave, but she hadn't even gotten anywhere near being realistic about what other changes a divorce would mean.

How would she support herself? Could she construct a new social life? Having gotten married right out of college, she'd never had to make her independent way in the world.

Allison had not actually named the emotional distance between Brad and herself as a problem, not until he had an affair, that is. It was what she came to call her Mighty Wake-up.

Years after her divorce, Allison reflected: "It was true that if I solved the emotional distance problem, there was a deeper one underneath. I was really fearful about answering the Who Am I question. I was worried there might not be anything in there or what was there wasn't acceptable or worthy. You've heard it a thousand times, but it's true: What you know and what is familiar and predictable is superior to what you don't know, even if it's the pits. The truth is, the more of the true Me I came to know, the more secure and empowered I felt. What I feared the most became my best friend. That's a continuing story that will last as long as I do."

Another big reason to resist making a change is the fear that once a door or window is opened a crack, the flood of old unfinished business will rush in to overwhelm us. When addressing a problem might reveal our failures and inadequacies, we'll defend the *status quo* to the hilt. When a problem seems beyond our ability to handle, we'll endlessly procrastinate in naming it for fear of what might lie underneath.

Pretending a life and avoiding a life are both stressful. That is not meant for any of us. God (Higher Power, the Universe, the Creator) is Love. Love is all around us. We deny love at our peril.

Love makes your soul crawl out from its hiding place.
                                               Zora Neale Hurston

---

Deciding Whom or What to Believe

Yet another unwelcome outcome of the rigid and regular enforcement of the Old Rules happens when family members lose the ability to tell what's real and what's not real. When members don't know what to believe, the leader can stir the pot to keep them distracted from her real goal of being in control and getting others to do things her way. The trouble is, in that environment, children spend far too much energy being vigilant and adaptive, that is, seeking a way to survive. They are not free to grow up with the confidence that comes with knowing what's real and dealing with it.

How does any child make sense of reality when he hears one message from the authority figures and what they say doesn't match the reality messages of his own sad and angry feelings? Are his feelings telling him what's true? Whom or what can he believe? When authority figures say one thing and do another, how is a child to know which message to believe, what's real, what is true? No wonder, then, that children grow up with feelings of uncertainty and mistrust of others–and tragically, of themselves.

Maybe the greatest confusion for a child to navigate occurs when the authority figures express their love for her, but her actual experience leans more toward feeling hollow rather than loved. The verbal expression of love is heard, but not necessarily felt as true. It gets qualified in the child's brain and heart as maybe true and maybe not. The love doesn't feel quite right. If the child's experience is that love is painful, or distant, the word *love* doesn't make sense. Love should not be painful.

She's in a quandary. If she believes and acts from her own reality, she's likely to be the outcast, named as the problem, or become the focus of the family's blame. *If it weren't for her, we'd be just fine.* If she believes what family members and others in the community say about her family, she may discount her own feelings, thereby deferring the job of defining her reality to others. If she tries to believe both her reality and that of others who see her situation differently, she either avoids making the decision about which reality to believe, or alternates between believing their version of reality and her own.

She may actually try so hard to make both realities into one that she risks a mental breakdown. To make a cognitive melding of two separate and very different realities is asking the brain to do the impossible. That's not saying that we can't hold opposites of the same thing in our brains. Take hard and soft. They can be thought of as opposites of one another. Both are true in themselves. It's quite a different challenge when we think it is possible to make two completely different ideas into one.

The closed system of family denial takes prisoners and the body count is high. The system is "closed" because the family system is close to impermeable. Incoming information that is at odds with the family's view of reality is summarily disqualified. Outgoing information about the family becomes more and more restricted. At some point, family members can be said to live on a tight little island of their own particular reality.

When what you see or experience as real and what I see or experience as real are pretty well congruent, our realities match. Where there is a discrepancy, there's likely to be a problem going on. The bigger the discrepancy in realities, the bigger the problem, or so it seems.

Of course, if you're old enough to do fact-checking, that's a good option. Facts from unbiased sources are crucial to deciding who and what to believe. Small children usually don't have that luxury.

Only when we are brave enough to explore the darkness will we discover the infinite power of our light.

Brené Brown

Silencing

Derrick Jensen[30] talks about silencing in this way. When a black belt denial of reality is going on, ask this question: Who benefits by keeping secrets or lying about their intentions? Who benefits from ridiculing, humiliating, and implicitly or explicitly threatening to expose or abandon others? The most common answer: the one with interests to protect, and if those interests were known, the person or persons in charge wouldn't be able to have their way. They want to protect themselves from being known for what they are doing. But they, themselves, know, at some level, that they have crossed a moral or legal boundary.

There are seen and unseen costs to having been silenced. What has happened didn't happen. What is happening now isn't happening. If we're accustomed to a context of denial, we can't see how it is used by others to keep control of whatever they're controlling. They use whatever combination of shame rules that works for them to keep others confused and stuck.

This is the kind of family climate created by the Old Rules and it isn't healthy for a soul and for a life.

The willingness to forget is the essence of silencing.

Derrick Jensen

Blinders, Blinders, Where are the Blinders?

Having learned the rudiments of denial by immersion in our families, we become accustomed to accommodating to it in other areas of our lives, as the following example illustrates.

A public official is supposed to be doing the country's and, presumably, the people's, business. Suppose she makes a secret deal that benefits friends, political supporters, and herself, a deal that would be contrary to the best interests of the majority of voters who elected her. The deal is exposed by a whistle-blower. What happens? A scramble to simultaneously blame and punish the whistle-blower and divert the spotlight from the guilty party, thereby relieving the miscreant from unwanted scrutiny. Just like at home.

Denial is a force that keeps others confused, so the one who needs power over others gets to maintain the *status quo*. Whoever is in denial unwittingly helps to maintain the status quo, as long, that is, as their denial of what's going on stays in place.

NEW RULE 7: Pay attention to what is true. Keep in touch with your own reality and check out your reality with others you trust. Move toward solving problems instead of denying them.

NOW WHAT? Replacing the Deny Reality Rule

Levels of Denial and Discounting

One meaning of *denial* is "a discounting of reality that keeps people from solving problems." Jacqui Schiff[31] identified four levels of denial/discounting that can help us understand how to support another person's coming out of denial.

The first-level of discounting is the most serious.

First level:	The problem doesn't exist.
	I'm lucky I'm so healthy.
Second level:	Recognizing the problem exists, but it has no impact on me.
	My back pain isn't so bad.
Third level:	The problem exists and impacts me, but I don't believe there are any solutions.
	I'll live with back pain; doctors only make it worse.
Fourth level:	I recognize there are solutions to the problem that impacts me, but I lack the personal power to put any one of them into effect.
	My friend got help for his bad back and it worked for him.
Empowerment:	There's a problem that impacts me and I have, or can gather, the personal power and support to solve it.
	I'll ask Jim for the name of his doctor tomorrow and call for an appointment.

It follows that if a person is at the fourth level of denial, coming out of denial and into the problem-solving light is a matter of gathering the personal resources to do so.

Let's say a family is in denial about their adolescent son's drug problem. Then they get a call from the hospital and learn that he was high when he drove his sports car into a bridge abutment. When life-threatening consequences present themselves, moving from first level discounting to the empowerment level can happen quickly. The family readily agrees to get treatment for their son right away.

Moving from one step to the next, and then to the next, toward acknowledging the problem and being ready to take action, defines a process of coming out of denial. Short of a traumatic "blow upside the head," moving through the levels of denial can be slow, especially in the eyes of loving bystanders who care about those so painfully trapped in it. For much more about the dynamics of denial, I recommend Chapters 20 through 23 in *Growing Up Again*.[32]

You know you are in love when you can't fall asleep
because reality is finally better than your dreams.

Dr. Seuss

Slipping the Hooks, Making the Turn

- If you didn't do the third exercise at the end of Chapter 6, do it now.

LIFE BEYOND SHAME: REWRITING THE RULES

- If it's safe to do so, keep asking questions in unclear situations.
- Whether for historical or current information, interview witnesses or observers who can provide you with their take on your situation.
- If you wish to give feedback to someone you care about, ask first if they're willing to hear it. Give them your reality without judgment, without a lecture, and without an assumption that they will hear you and/or be grateful. Begin with a small piece and resist the urge to dump your load in one fell swoop.
- If you see denial working in the lives of others, take a look to see how it might be working in your own. Denial is sneaky. Give yourself a pat on the back for taking back personal power you may have given up.

Everything is energy and that's all there is to it. Match the frequency of the reality you want and you cannot help but get that reality. It can be no other way. This is not philosophy. This is physics.

Albert Einstein

Moving On

The first six rules consist of human responses to the inhumane expectations that are called out in the first rule, which tells us to do what's not only unwise, but impossible. Denial is the last of the shame rules and the one that keeps the others in place. *What's going on is not going on. No problem here! Look over there! The rules don't exist!*

That which we witness, we are forever changed by,
and once witnessed we can never go back.

Angeles Arrien

CHAPTER ELEVEN

EVERYDAY SHAME

Responding to Feeling Shamed

Shame Happens. Here is one way to move through the first moments of feeling ashamed. Note that feeling shamed by a store clerk doesn't carry the same importance as feeling shamed by someone close to you. You can walk away from the clerk more easily than you can walk away from someone close to you!

If the relationship is one of value to you, first of all, pay attention to the trigger you feel in your body. Realize your sensitivity in the situation and let a spirit of calm wash over you. If your feelings are flooding your ability to think, say so and postpone the conversation—but not too much later, or it might never take place.

Having this conversation tests our vulnerability and how much we've come to understand about ourselves. The following process is a way of having a conversation about a shame-triggering situation:

1. Although it's your feelings that signal what's going on, consciously switch out of your feelings and into a thinking mode. Feelings of shame often mean we're also feeling unsafe or insecure. An animal who is being chased by another animal who considers him food needs his thinking to get himself to a safer place! Practice telling your brain to switch from feeling to thinking, back and forth, so you understand the difference between the two. You need your thinking when you're called upon to protect yourself.

2. Ask the other person "Are you willing to talk to me (about what happened)?" If yes, ask for clarification, more information, particularly focused on the specifics of the situation where the conflict or affront originated. Resist the urge to jump to conclusions. You are simply on a fact-finding mission. If the other person makes a derailing or distracting comment, ask that you stick to this one incident at hand. One at a time!

3. Listen with empathy to the other person. If you hear a place where you have some responsibility for the problem, acknowledge it and apologize, if necessary. Ask the other person to hear your experience of the situation.

4. Are you satisfied you have untangled the situation that gave rise to your feeling shamed? What about the other person?

5. Decision time. Are you both willing to move ahead? Reconnect? Repair any damage? Decide what's next.

6. Make a new agreement, carry through, and carry on.

Steps 1 and 2 are the WHAT? of the problem. Steps 3 and 4 get at the SO WHAT? What did the situation mean to each person?

Steps 5 and 6 are the NOW WHAT? This might be a resolution of the problem (shaming). The outcome of a conversation like this can make the limits of a relationship clearer. It can also lead to seeing someone for help.

Keep the New Rules in mind.

People make mistakes. Healthy people accept responsibility for their words and actions. They get the data their feelings provide. They recognize that secrets contaminate relationships. They strive to be accountable. They remember the limits of what they can control. As you can, move your interactions in that direction.

Recognizing When You May Have Shamed Others

Shame and shaming is learned. It's what we know. Words can come out in an instant and in an unwanted way. Interrupting a pattern of shaming others inadvertently has two aspects. First, we're uncomfortable, disturbed. We recognize we said or did something we regret and want to take it back. *I'm sorry. I'd like to try again.* Second, the other person is disturbed. If they don't say something, how will we know? Of course we can always check it out, but here are some signals:

1. Watch for body clues to shame, particularly disengagement from eye contact, cutting off contact, shutting down.
2. Check your perception with the receiving person, apologize, and reiterate your intention not to be shaming of others.
3. If you need to make amends or restitution, do so, or state your intention to do so. We can express how we value and wish to keep the relationship.

4. Express how you envision this relationship down the road.

5. Thank the other for being open to what you are trying and practicing to do differently.

So much of shaming is inadvertent. We don't know what will hook another person until his shame reaction occurs. We may also miss the cues because they can be so very subtle. All we can do is our best. After learning about shaming, any of us can take steps to look at our own relationships with shame and shaming. Then we will be more aware and understanding of others.

Love isn't finding a perfect person.
It's seeing an imperfect person perfectly,

Sam Keen

The Wisdom of Learning When to Duck

Life is scary for people in places that run according to the Old Rules, and with good reason. At any moment, a leader can pull a switcheroo or blame the blameless. The controller can unpredictably pull a 180-degree turn when it suits their purpose and shift blame for any negative fallout to the nearest innocent person. Living under such a continual threat is anything but safe. Life becomes constantly uncertain. Brilliantly adaptable family members have little recourse but to develop ways to get along and stay out of the line of fire.

Why would we want to expose ourselves to ridicule and abandonment in a system that expects us to *be* perfect and *do* perfectly? Why wouldn't we stay defended? A friend long ago said of his former wife, "She had a way of annihilating me." Why would he risk sticking his neck out if he expected to be annihilated? Wouldn't it be far smarter to keep his Light at least partially hidden, and safe, under a bushel?

Here's the truth: Stepping back to carefully assess a situation, watching and observing the dynamics before deciding what's in our best interests is a serviceable skill. It's very hard to observe what's going on if we're right in the thick of it. We can gain invaluable information about relationships and how the Old Rules system works by watching thoughtfully so we know when and how we want to stick our necks out.

This is true, however, only when ducking is an option.

Who Are You, Pilgrim?

Newly divorced, Sarah knew she wanted to feel more connected. And she wanted more joy in her life. Watching couples who seemed to like being together, and people who seemed to genuinely enjoy one another, left her feeling that something was missing. She knew the "something" was her. "I feel so awkward, like I'm in a pool and they're on the other side. I want to join them, but I don't know how to get there. The others seem so much more at ease with themselves than I do. They're not playing a game, they're in the game."

What were they doing that she wasn't doing?

Swallowing her pride, she finally took herself to a therapist who asked, "Why are you here? What would you like to be better about your life?"

"I don't know." said Sarah. "I'm watching what I call The Happy Ones *closely and compared to them, I'm a loser. They seem so comfortable and I feel awkward and out of place." The therapist waited.*

Sarah's shoulders dropped. Another one of those awful times when the truth she feared to acknowledge, let alone speak, flashed in front of her eyes. She quickly said something else, something that was true but that wasn't her basic truth. She knew her deepest secret and didn't want to reveal it for what it said about her.

Then it just rushed out of her mouth! "I think I don't deserve to be connected. I don't deserve to be happy. I don't deserve to be loved. I'm really lonely inside even though I don't think I look like I am."

The therapist spoke again. "I'd like to suggest we start our work by finding out more about how you connect with yourself. She's the one you need to be close to. She's the one that others want to know. She's the one she takes wherever she goes, and I, for one, would like to get to know her. Are you game?"

To this day, Sarah says she doesn't know what made her say yes.

When you see someone putting on his Big Boots, you can be pretty sure that an Adventure is going to happen.

A.A. Milne

Be the One You Are
By Kim Stafford

I want to say to those I love, be the one you are. Be odd, and yourself. Be the one who doesn't get it, if you don't, or the one who gets it when no one else does, or the one who speaks with silence if you must. You are the only one who knows.

Be the scarlet leaf swiveling single in the dark-green tree. Be the goose that veers by the heart compass when the flock does not. Be the road that turns away from the valley, climbs the ridge instead, threads chaotic fog to tunnel through blooming trees at the crest. Be the old woman who wears purple, or the young one. Don't wait. Don't put it off. Be the pedestrian who lifts her face and laughs at rain as others trudge, head down and glum, at 5 p.m. You know the secret. The secret is a felt sense of life, a tingling. Take off its mask. No one can make this happen for you.

Chapter Twelve

AFTER WORDS

If you are depressed, you are living in the past.
If you are anxious, you are living in the future.
If you are at peace, you are living in the present.

Lao Tzu

Staying Awake, Staying Curious, Staying Compassionate

A strong, capable, and vibrant woman in her 60's felt there had always been some unseen force holding her back. An internal voice told her she should be more, so much more.

She had never thought of her family in the light of shame. Her family of origin was upper middle class. Her father was college-educated and a lifelong teacher. The family experienced some thin economic times, but all in all, no one went without what they needed.

As she read the manuscript of this book, she recognized the

shame rules as only *faint assumptions*. We both laughed about her being Norwegian. With a twinkle in her eye she said, "You know how reserved Norwegians are!" Chris wrote her story.

I realized I had a degree of basic insecurity that kept me from accepting myself and my talents when I knew I wanted to share them. I play the violin. I ride horses. I have written a book. Yet I have not claimed any one of those as an authentic expression of me – of who I am. I blow off the 50+ years I played the violin in orchestras around the world. After being challenged by a therapist, I am now able to say "I am a proficient violinist who plays the chamber music I love with my friends on a weekly basis. I may not be a touring soloist or play in a big city professional orchestra, but I have enough skill to enjoy what I do."

I began to think differently about myself and my horseback riding. I may not be an Olympic dressage rider, but I ride well enough to enjoy doing competitive musical rides on my horse, and I continue to learn at my own level. I may think I'm not really a writer, yet I've produced a book with an important message, and I need to not hide that under my too-familiar bushel. I may not think I am an artist, but I have produced sketches for my book that enhance the message. I may not be showing professionally in galleries, but I can produce what I need to augment my manuscript and delight me.

I can already feel some additional energy around who I am when I don't struggle to cover myself in shadow. Seeing myself as competent and not "less than" is a work in progress. I'm mindful there is a difference between arrogance and acceptance. I don't want to cross the line of self-importance into arrogance, yet I do want to be able to step out into the world feeling content with who I am and not apologizing for myself.

This whole experience is somewhat of a surprise for me. I wasn't aware I had this baggage slowing me down from being who I am meant to be in this world. I am grateful for the lights coming on, even at my age, so I can redefine myself for me.

In a conversation that took place well after she wrote her story, Chris is still discovering ways the Old Rules affected her thinking even though her family "didn't have any of the usual obvious problems like abuse or violence or addiction."

I reminded her that, like the rest of us, she grew up in a culture that is steeped in the shame rules. "Your family was enculturated to them pretty much like everyone else. Maybe that's all it took for you to think that you were not enough."

My friend got quiet. I waited. Then she said, *My dad had a lot of medical problems when I was growing up. I remember being a little ashamed because he wasn't like my friends' dads. There were lots of things we didn't take part in because of his limitations. Mother and Dad were really good people whom I love and who love me. I guess I don't need to dig for the whys of past shame in my life as much as I'm interested in moving into believing the New Rules now. And seeing myself a little differently.*

Shame and Pride, Pride and Joy

Pride in one's self and one's accomplishments is the polar opposite of shame. So says Donald L. Nathanson in *Shame and Pride: Affect, Sex, and the Birth of the Self.*

Pride. The sense of one's own proper dignity or value. Self-respect.

If you heard, as I did growing up, that "pride goeth before

a fall (destruction)" and "self-praise stinks," were we wrong to conclude that being proud of our accomplishments wasn't a good thing? *Don't show you're better than anyone else. Don't win the race because it makes other people feel bad. You can win the spelling bee but it will cost you some friends.* What? Is that an admonishment to keep my light under a bushel? Is it a reminder that there's a target on my back or a reminder that I should compare myself to somebody else and find myself lacking? If life is a case of win or lose, then I must be a loser. My jealousy of the winner's joy is tied to feeling cut off from my own.

I don't remember hearing "I'm proud of what you've accomplished!" There were occasions when I overheard Mother telling Aunt Evelyn about my accomplishment, but she never told *me*. If she did, I didn't hear it. I told this story as I taught about the dynamics of self-esteem in a college class. The last sentence of my story was, "In my family, you'd think if someone said something good about you directly *to* you, the world would explode. I wonder what that's about."

After class, a student approached. "I am the Godmother of my niece. At her baptism in a Greek Orthodox ceremony, the priest gazed at the baby in his arms. Smiling tenderly, he spoke about how beautiful she was and how full of God's promise. Then he turned his head to the side and with lips pursed, faked spitting three times, then smoothly went on with what came next."

"Do you understand the meaning of spitting three times in a baptism ceremony?" I asked.

She said, "It comes from way back. Something about spitting three times to ward off the Evil Eye."

So that's it! Words of pride were words of danger? Does that mean that feeling "full of ourselves" makes us vulnerable to a primeval lurking dread lying deep in the human psyche?

Here's the rub. If pride is the polar opposite of shame, I'd like to be able to genuinely and fully feel proud of making a sincere effort. I want to be unreservedly proud of going the extra mile for a friend, or making a beautiful bookshelf, or cooking a delicious Thanksgiving dinner, or being a considerate, kind human being. **Feeling that pride fully is pure joy.**

Those of us who challenge the shame rules, can be mindful that there's a difference between pride and haughtiness. Haughtiness tends toward pomposity and conceitedness. Feeling pride in oneself is that wonderful sense of one's own dignity and value and being proud of one's sincere efforts. *That is the very essence of joy. I'm okay. I am who I am. I belong here. I'm confident in the abilities I have. I'm a loving human being and I'm growing.*

Getting Comfortable with the New Rules

Switching out the shame rules for pride rules is the means for changing humiliation into joy. Once we see how the shame-based rules work, we've taken a first step. The next step is to figure out what to do about how they're working in our lives right now. Last, if we choose to do so, we can apply the New Rules persistently enough so they become automatic.

It takes diligence, patience, persistence, and celebration when we're learning something new and letting go of something old. Here is a way of explaining this most wonderful process of changing ~ how the new and unfamiliar becomes the old and automatic.[33]

We begin with being *unconsciously incompetent.* We're frustrated but unaware. Being incompetent isn't our choice; it is simply a blind spot. We don't have the information we need to suggest another way of doing things. When we're first presented with a new way of thinking or a new behavior, we become aware of our incompetence. "Why didn't somebody tell me?" We know we've arrived at the stage of being *consciously incompetent.*

As we head toward a new behavior, we need to try it out. We notice and fine-tune what works and what doesn't as we go along. Whoopee! We're on our way to being *consciously competent.* Then, one fine day, we realize we've become *unconsciously competent.* We've integrated the once-new behavior into our automatic bank and have ourselves a new normal. "Voilà!"

Not that we'll never retreat to a familiar but unwanted behavior, but we know how to get back to the wanted one and keep on going. *I'm sorry. I didn't like the way that came out of my mouth. I'd like to try again.* And do it.

Can I Do This?

You won't know if you can do it unless you try. Pick the one area or idea that interests you the most. There's a swarm of places to begin. Here are a few to get your thinking moving:

Maybe it's working on just one rule by observing and recognizing how the rule works in the lives and interactions of others, or begin with yourself, if you feel ready. Maybe it's becoming aware of your words and reactions to the behavior of others and working to avoid what might be shaming to you. Maybe it's dealing with being blamed or blaming others. Maybe it's substituting the word *responsibility* for *blame*, from *Who's to blame?* to *Who's responsible for what?* Maybe it's identifying your shame hooks and thinking about their origins. Maybe it's becoming more aware of irresponsible language and picking one thing to try out for yourself. Maybe it's looking for more information from the rich buffet of resources to be found on the Internet or asking friends for recommendations.

Start with what's right in front of you, with what's on your plate at the moment. Let yourself know what you know.

The Scarecrow watched the Woodsman
while he worked and said to him
"I cannot think why this wall is here nor what it is made of."
"Rest your brains and do not worry about
the wall," replied the Woodsman.
"When we have climbed over it we shall
know what is on the other side."

L. Frank Baum

Forgiveness

We've all taken passed-on, unintended shaming by others into ourselves. We've defined our young selves by what our personal authority figures said or did, or by the unfriendly circumstances into which we were born. In other words, any shame we carry as part of our operating system first belonged to someone else. Their shaming of us wasn't fair. It wasn't right.

Why forgive? To dwell on what happened and to avoid

grieving what *should have been* keeps us stuck. Continuing to blame them unknowingly keeps resentment going. Our energy is misplaced. The wrongdoer's behavior continues to control us in present time! And it's taking care of the wrongdoer's pain. That pain rightfully belongs to those who didn't do this work and transferred their pain to us. Never mind that we loved them or wanted to love them and be loved back. Give the painful energy back. Use a giving-back ritual, if you like. Detoxify any negative leftover energy. Most of all, forgive yourself. We're all humans having a human experience.

Forgiveness is essential, not only to happiness, but to better health. There are really only two steps in the process: grieving and letting go. M. Scott Peck[34] added this idea. We need to be like a judge. We must first find the offender(s) guilty before we are free to forgive them.

When we feel wronged, we need to grieve what we wanted and didn't get. Grieving is allowing ourselves to feel all the anger, hurt, and possibly betrayal, associated with the original pain. Lean into the process, feel the feelings, think of the meanings of the loss or absence to you.

How do we let go? By being mindful, remembering that letting go frees you to move on with your life. Instead of continuing to focus on old anger, focus on your spirit of kindness and stay present with what you're grateful for now.

Out of understanding comes every form of love.

Sherwin Newland

Amends and Restitution

Forgiveness has two best friends: the willingness to make amends and doing acts of restitution. "Making amends" means changing for the better. It's literally an add-on. Amends round out the deal after we've acknowledged our behavior and taken responsibility for our part. Making amends (changing for the better) is our commitment to stop doing the harm that resulted from our behavior in the first place.

Restitution is the act of giving back something we've taken. In the broadcast industry, if an advertisement doesn't play correctly or is botched in some way, the station does a "make good" by playing it again at another time and without charge. Restitution is a make-good. It's intended to repair harm, loss, or injury in a way that restores wholeness.

Focus on This: Look for the Goodness

Cultural anthropologist Angeles Arrien said this: "Rarely do we realize that if we simply take time to marvel at life's gifts and give thanks for them, we activate stunning opportunities to increase their influence in our lives." Many have spoken of what seems to be a universal principle: **What you focus on, expands.** Focus on worry, get more worry. Focus on scarcity, get more scarcity. Focus on war, get more war. Focus on goodness, get more goodness. Focus on love, expand your loving.

Look around you for the Good. Look for what touches your heart. Watch for what brings a tear of celebration or longing to your eye, and a smile to your heart–like some of these:

- The reaction of a soldier's children to his surprise homecoming.
- The prison inmates who perform a play about the betrayal of Jesus and play the parts with the raw truth and passion born of their own knowing.
- A toddler who puts a comforting arm around a playmate who's having a hard time.
- A crew who makes lunches for homeless or low-income kids and doesn't count how many lunches the kids take with them for the hungry ones at home.
- A man who offers to help raise money to cover the medical expenses of a friend's daughter.
- A man who uses the quiet strength of his presence to stop the humiliation of others.
- Watching the unaffected behaviors of toddlers as they interact and explore.
- Flash mobs that touch our humanity.
- A song. A book. Birds. Flowers. Truth.
- The warmth of caring for your Light.
- Gazing into the eyes of a baby.
- And so much more...

For beautiful eyes, look for the good in others;
for beautiful lips, speak only words of kindness;
and for poise, walk with the knowledge that you are never alone.

Audrey Hepburn

Destinations

If you know why you've chosen your destination, you will get there. There will be people on your way who invite you to change your destination. There will be people on your way whose smiles reward your efforts. The choice of destinations is yours.

On your journey, you will meet a sense of uncertainty. What behavior could be riskier than being who you are? The better question is this: What behavior could be riskier than *not* being who you are? Ask yourself how you can feel the feelings and move forward anyway. On your journey, squalls will show up. Hold steady. Stay your course. The squalls will pass. All the way along your journey, appreciate the milestones. Smile at your expanding heart. It's okay to enjoy your progress! If you're lucky, you will arrive at your final destination having little to regret and much for which to be grateful.

_____

If your ship doesn't float, don't try explaining it to the ocean.

Julien Puzey

_____

Moving On

As you set out on this adventure, give yourself permission to buddy up with a fellow traveler. Pick someone whose reality checks you trust. Grow together and celebrate what works.

Pay attention to your life.

Smile a lot.

Just remember: Change like a sailboat. Respect your turning radius. The changes you make are for real and for the long haul.

And yes, you can do this. More than that, you deserve to make your life what it's meant to be and what you want it to be. All the New Rules suggest taking better care of yourself. It just so happens that the better care you take of yourself, the better care (love) you can give and share with others.

---

the most visible creators I know of are those artists
whose medium is life itself.
the ones who express the inexpressible
without brush, hammer, clay or guitar.
they neither paint nor sculpt – their medium is being.
whatever their presence touches has increased life.
they see and don't have to draw.
they are the artists of being alive....

J. Stone

APPENDIX A

NURTURE & STRUCTURE CHARTS

THE NURTURE CHART, page 1

Joy, hope, self-confidence, and self-esteem grow from care and support. Despair, joylessness, and loneliness flow from abuse, conditional care, overindulgence, and neglect.

ABUSE	CONDITIONAL CARE	ASSERTIVE CARE

Characteristics:

Abuse involves relating to a child by assault, physical or psychological invasion, direct or indirect "don't be" messages. Abuse negates the child's needs.	Conditional care requires the child to earn care or pay for care in some way. The care the parent gives the child is based on the parent's needs and expectations, not on the child's needs.	Assertive care recognizes the child and the child's needs. The parent decides to nurture in this way because it is helpful to the child, responsive to the child's needs, and appropriate to the circumstance. It is comforting and loving. It is freely given.

Example: School-age child has a badly scraped arm.

Parent does not care for wounds. Says, "Stop sniffling or I'll give you something to cry about." Yells at or shakes the child.	Parent says, "Stop crying or I won't bandage your arm."	Parent cares for the wound in a loving way. Says, "Your arm is scraped! I'm sorry."

Children May Hear the Following Underlying Messages:

You don't count. Your needs don't count. You are not lovable. You don't deserve to exist. To get what you need, you must expect pain.	I matter and you don't. Your needs and feelings don't count. You can have care as long as you earn it. Don't believe you are lovable; you have to earn love.	I love you and you are lovable. You are important. Your needs are important. I care for you willingly.

Common Responses of Children:

Pain in the heart, as well as pain in the scraped arm. Fear, terror, rage, withdrawal, loneliness, despair, shame, confusion about reality.	Pain in the heart, as well as pain in the scraped arm. Fear, terror, anger, mistrust of own perceptions, shame, feelings of inadequacy, suspicious of love.	Pain in the arm and warmth in the heart. Feels comforted, accepted, important, satisfied, relieved, secure, safe, loved.

Decisions Often Made by Children:

I am not powerful. I deserve to die, or the reverse, I will live in spite of them. It's my fault, or I'll blame everything on others. I'll be good, or I'll be bad. Big people get to abuse, or I can abuse those smaller than I am, or I will never abuse. I won't feel or have needs. Love does not exist. I am alone; I keep emotional distance from, and don't trust, others. I blame or strike or leave first.	I am what I do. I must strive to please. Big people get what they want. I can never do enough. I must be perfect. I don't deserve love. There is a scarcity of love. I must be strong. Love obligates me and is costly. I don't trust. I do keep emotional distance, run away, or blame others.	I am important. I deserve care. It's okay to ask for what I need. I belong here. I am loved. Others can be trusted and relied upon. I can know what I need. It's okay to be dependent at times.

THE NURTURE CHART, page 2

SUPPORTIVE CARE   OVERINDULGENCE   NEGLECT

Characteristics:

Supportive care recognizes the child and the child's needs. It is care the child is free to accept or reject. It offers help, comfort, and love. It stimulates children to think and to do what they are capable of doing for themselves.	Overindulgence is a sticky, patronizing kind of care. It promotes continuing dependence on the parent and teaches the child not to think independently and not to be responsible for self or to others.	Neglect is passive abuse. It is lack of emotional or physical stimulation and recognition by parents who are unavailable or who ignore the needs of the child. These parents may be "there, but not there."

Example: School-age child has a badly scraped arm.

[Parent has already taught child how to clean a scrape.] Says in a concerned and loving tone, "I see you've scraped your arm. Does it hurt? Do you want to take care of it yourself or would you like some help from me?" Offers a hug.	Parent rushes to child. Says, "Oh, look at your arm, you poor thing. That really stings! I'll bandage it. Go and lie down in front of the television and I'll do your chores for you."	Parent ignores the scrape. Says, "Don't bother me."

Children May Hear the Following Underlying Messages:

I love you, you are lovable. You are capable. I am willing to care for you. Ask for what you need. Your welfare is important to me. I am separate from you. I trust you to think and make judgments in your own best interests.	Don't grow up. Don't be who you are (capable). My needs are more important than yours (or) your needs are more important than mine. You don't need to care for yourself; someone will care for you.	Don't expect to be recognized. Your needs are not important. You are not important. You do not deserve to exist. Expect to suffer to get what you need. Be confused about reality.

Common Responses of Children:

Pain in the arm and a heart filled with confidence. Child feels cared for, comforted, challenged, secure, and trustworthy.	Pain in the arm and uncertainty in the heart. Self-centered satisfaction, temporary comfort, self-righteousness. Later on: confusion, woefulness, helplessness, obligation, resentment, defensiveness, and shame. Not knowing what is enough.	Pain in the heart, as well as pain in the scraped arm. Feelings of abandonment, fear, shame, rage, hopelessness, helplessness, abject disappointment.

Decisions Often Made by Children:

I am loved. I can know what I need. I am capable. I can be powerful. I am not alone. It's okay to ask for help. I am both separate and connected. I can decide when to be dependent and when to be independent.	I am not capable. I don't have to be competent. I don't have to know what I need, think, or feel. Other people are obligated to take care of me. I don't have to grow up. I must be loyal to my indulging parent. To get my needs met, I manipulate or play a victim role. It's okay to be self-centered. Later on: be wary and don't trust.	I don't really know who I am or what's right. I am not important. I am not lovable. I die alone or survive on my own. It isn't possible or safe to get close, to trust, or to ask for help. I do not deserve help. What I do doesn't count if someone has to help me. Life is hard.

THE STRUCTURE CHART, page 1

Children internalize protection, safety, freedom, success, and self-esteem from nonnegotiable rules and negotiable rules. Despair and failure come from rigidity, criticism, marshmallowing, and abandonment.

RIGIDITY ◩	CRITICISM ⬚	NON-NEGOTIABLE ◼ RULES
Characteristics:		
Rigidity, supposedly for the child's welfare, springs from fear. It consists of old rules "written in concrete" sometime in the past and usually for someone else. These rules often ignore the developmental tasks of the child. Rigidity threatens abuse or withdrawal of love to enforce compliance; it doesn't believe children should have a say in working things out.	Criticism labels the person with bad names rather than setting standards for acceptable behavior. Criticism often includes global words such as "never" and "always." It negates children and tells them how to fail. Ridicule is a devastating form of criticism that humiliates and invites contemptuous laughter from others.	Nonnegotiable rules are rules that must be followed. Children count on these rules to put order in their lives, to provide safety and security, to help them know who they are, to help them make decisions, and to build their own self-esteem. Even though nonnegotiable rules are firmly set and firmly enforced, they are not "rigid" and can be rewritten for the welfare of the family and its members.
Example: Thirteen-year-old drank alcohol.		
Parent says, "If you ever touch alcohol again, don't bother coming home."	Mother says, "You're always doing something stupid. Now you are drinking. You're just like your dad."	Parent says, "You may not drink alcohol until you reach the legal age. We expect you to honor this rule. If you do not honor the rule, there will be very tough consequences."
Children May Hear the Following Underlying Messages:		
You are not important. Don't think. Don't be. Don't exist. You will be punished or abandoned if you make a mistake. Don't trust your own competence.	Don't be who you are. Don't be successful. Don't be capable. You are not lovable.	Your welfare and safety are important. Your parents expect you to be law abiding. Your parents are willing to be responsible and enforce the rules.
Common Responses of Children:		
Feels oppressed, distanced, angry or rageful, scared, hopeless, imperfect, discounted, mistrusted, abandoned, no-good, powerless.	Feels powerless and diminished, rejected, hurt, humiliated, squashed, angry or rageful, unimportant, inadequate, scared, discounted.	Feels safe, cared for, powerful, helped, responsible, confident, accounted for. May feel frustrated, irritated, and resistant at times. Learns to follow rules and be responsible.
Decisions Often Made by Children:		
Rules are more important than my needs. I am not wanted. My parents don't care about me. I will let others think for me. I will comply, rebel, or withdraw. I will blame myself.	I'm supposed to know what I don't know. I won't ask for help. I will try harder, be strong, be perfect. If I don't do things right, I am a bad person. I can't be good enough. I am hopeless. Why bother?	There are some rules I have to follow. I can learn from my mistakes. I am a good person. I'm lovable and capable. They care about me and take care of me.

THE STRUCTURE CHART, page 2

NEGOTIABLE RULES

Characteristics:

Negotiable rules teach children how to think clearly and to solve problems, helping them raise their self-esteem. These rules are negotiated. The process of negotiating provides children an opportunity to argue and hassle with parents, learn about the relevancy of rules, assess data on which to base decisions, and learn to be increasingly responsible for themselves.

Example: Thirteen-year-old drank alcohol.

Parent says, "There are kids whose number one priority is drinking. When do you think it is okay to be with kids who drink? How can you find kids who don't drink so you don't spend all of your free time with the ones who are drinking?"

Children May Hear the Following Underlying Messages:

You can think, negotiate, and initiate. Your needs are important and others' needs are important. You must deal with how things really are. You are expected to be powerful in positive ways for yourself and others.

Common Responses of Children:

Feels respected, cared for, listened to, powerful, important, loved, intelligent, safe, and sometimes frustrated. Learns to evaluate rules and participate in the making of rules as well as to follow rules and be responsible.

Decisions Often Made by Children:

It's okay for me to grow up and still be dependent at times. I can think things through and ask others to think with me. I continually expand my ability to be responsible and competent.

MARSHMALLOW

Marshmallow parenting grants freedom without demanding responsibility in return. It sounds supportive, but it implies the child does not have to or is not capable of following rules. It discounts the child's ability and gives the child permission to be irresponsible and to fail, to be helpless and hopeless. At the same time, it lets the parent look good or play the martyr or feel in control.

Parent says, "If all the kids drink, I suppose you can," or "You're too young to drink and drive, so you can have a kegger here," or "Kids will be kids!"

Don't be competent or responsible. Don't be who you are. Don't grow up. You can have your way and be obnoxious and get by with it. I need to continue taking care of you. My needs are more important than your needs.

Feels patronized and encouraged not to grow up, remains incompetent in order to please parent. Feels unsafe, undermined, crazy, manipulated, discounted, unloved, unsatisfied, and angry.

I must take care of other people's feelings and needs, or I don't need to care about anyone but me. I am not capable of learning how to value and take care of myself. If help is offered, I mistrust it or at least expect to pay a price for it, but I don't expect helpful structure from others.

ABANDONMENT

Abandonment consists of lack of rules, protection, and contact. It tells children that adults are not available for them. If teasing is used when a child needs structure or approval, that teasing constitutes abandonment.

Parents says, "I don't want to talk about it." Parent is not available (either physically or emotionally), is drunk or mentally ill, or ignores or teases the child.

I am not willing to care for you. I don't want you. Your needs are not important, mine are. No one is here for you. You don't exist.

Feels scared, terrified, hurt, angry or rageful, rejected, discounted, baffled, unimportant, upset. Perhaps suicidal.

Don't ask for or expect help. No one cares. If I am to survive, I will have to do it by myself. If help is offered, mistrust it. Help and trust are jokes.

233

APPENDIX B

AFFIRMATIONS

USING AFFIRMATIONS TO REINFORCE
CHANGING TO NEW RULES THINKING

Challenge your **DO IT RIGHT** beliefs with the following statements. Read, say, post on your mirror, and ask another to say them to you. Then choose one statement from each list that makes the best message from you to yourself.

Core statement: You can make healthy decisions about your experiences.

I'm glad you're alive.

I'm glad you are you.

I love who you are.

You can do things as many times as you need to.

You can find a way of doing things that works for you.

You can know what you need and ask for help.

Challenge your early beliefs about **BLAME** and blaming by checking these true statements with what you believe now. Choose one statement from each list that makes the best message from you to yourself.

Core statement: You can be responsible for your needs and behavior.

Your needs and safety are important.

You can think before you say yes or no and learn from your mistakes

You can trust your inner wisdom.

You can find out the results of your behavior.

I love who you are.

You can explore who you are and find out who other people are.

Challenge your early beliefs about the integrity of your **FEELINGS.** Choose one statement from each list that makes the best message from you to yourself.

Core statement: You can feel all your feelings.

All of your feelings are okay with me.

You can think and feel at the same time.

I celebrate that you are alive.

You can learn to think for yourself and others can think for themselves.

I love you just as you are.　　　It's okay for you to be
angry and not hurt yourself
or others.

Challenge your early beliefs about keeping **SECRETS** that, if known, would help you improve the quality of your life. Choose one statement from each list that makes the best message from you to yourself.

Core statement: You can know what you know.

You can trust your intuition
to help you know what to
believe and what to do.

You can think for yourself
and others can think for
themselves.

You can say your hellos and
goodbyes to people, roles,
dreams, and decisions.

You can learn when and
how to disagree.

My love is always with
you. I trust you will get the
support you need.

Challenge your early beliefs about **ACCOUNTABILITY**...about being able to count on someone else and yourself. Choose one statement from each list that makes the best message for you to give yourself now.

Core statement: You can be responsible for each of your commitments.

You can be powerful and ask for help at the same time.

You can build and develop your own interests, relationships and causes.

Your love matures and expands.

You can learn the rules that help you live with others.

You can know who you are and learn and practice the skills for independence.

You can be creative, competent, productive, and joyful.

Challenge your early beliefs about being in **CONTROL** or being controlled. Choose one statement from each list to develop a message that makes better sense to you now.

Core statement: I'm glad you're starting to think for yourself.

You can be uniquely yourself and honor the uniqueness of others.

You can try out different roles and ways of being powerful.

I like to watch you initiate and grow and learn.

You can say no and push and test limits as much as you need to.

You can separate from ideas that don't work for you and I will continue to love you.

You can think for yourself and get help instead of staying in distress.

Challenge yourself to tell when to **DENY** and when denial holds you back. Choose one statement from each list to construct a message you can give to yourself.

Core statement: You can learn what is pretend and what is real.

Your needs are important.

You can find a way of doing things that works for you.

You deserve the support you need.

You can learn to use old skills in new ways.

You can trust your inner wisdom.

You can learn when and how to disagree.

APPENDIX C

RULES POSTERS

OLD RULES POSTER

DO AND BE RIGHT

Be morally, intellectually and socially right. Don't make mistakes. Regard yourself and others harshly for errors in judgment and performance.

BLAME

When you make a mistake or get blamed for something, pass the blame elsewhere.

IGNORE YOUR FEELINGS

Do not acknowledge your feelings about what's going on.

KEEP SECRETS

Do not raise the issue or ask questions about whatever might jeopardize the status quo.

BE UNCLEAR AND UNACCOUNTABLE

Don't communicate clearly. Be wary of commitments, promises, and agreements.

BE IN CONTROL

Manipulate, threaten, coerce and use whatever works to get what you need.

DENY REALITY

What's going on is not going on. Accept discrepant behaviors and occurrences as normal.

Credit to the St. Paul (MN) Family Therapy Institute for identifying these dynamics. See _Facing Shame: Families in Recovery,_ Fossum and Mason, W.W. Norton, 1986 Copyright: Connie Dawson, Ph.D. conniedawson.com Permission to reproduce this page for educational purposes only.

NEW RULES POSTER

LEARN,

And then learn again from your mistakes.

ACCEPT RESPONSIBILITY

For your decisions and behaviors.

PAY ATTENTION TO YOUR FEELINGS.

Acknowledge your feelings and use the information they provide to identify what you need.

TELL YOUR TRUTH

In the most respectful and likely receivable way, after first recognizing your own.

BE CLEAR AND ACCOUNTABLE FOR YOUR AGREEMENTS AND TO YOUR COMMITMENTS.

ASK FOR WHAT YOU NEED.

Be willing to negotiate. Be responsible *for* yourself and *to* others.

PAY ATTENTION TO WHAT IS TRUE.

Keep in touch with your own reality and check out your reality with others you trust. Move toward solving problems instead of denying them.

APPENDIX D

WORKSHEETS

Connecting Feelings to Needs

Record your feelings in the first column, what triggered them in the second column and in the third column, write what you need. In the fourth column, write how you might respond to the triggering experience, claiming what you need.

FEELING(S)	TRIGGER	NEED	RESPONSE
Mad	My partner ridiculed the special dinner I made	Respect	Say, *I don't respond to ridicule. Find another way to communicate your likes and dislikes.*

Permission to reproduce for educational purposes

Secrets and Lies

Identifying the personal impact of a deception can help to decide if a secret needs to be kept. In this worksheet, write an example for each of the four categories in the first column. In the second column, note the situation or context of the secret or lie. Then focus particularly on the impact of having kept the secret or told the lie.

SECRET/LIE	THE SITUATION	IMPACT
Write *a secret you keep. You may have told this secret to one other person. Use symbols if you would rather not write the words.*		
Write *something you know about someone else and are withholding. Assume that if they knew what you know, they might use the information to improve their quality of life.*		
Write *a lie you've told recently.*		
Write *a lie you tell yourself.*		

Permission to reproduce for educational purposes.

ENDNOTES

1   Merle A. Fossum and Marilyn J. Mason wrote *Facing Shame: Families in Recovery* which was published in 1986 (W.W. Norton & Co., New York). I heard Dr. Mason's lecture in 1980, when the "rules" and their articulation were under development. I have used the rules governing family interactions as they were presented then. I am indebted to Drs. Fossum and Mason for their recognition and articulation of the dynamic pattern of interaction in families whose systems can be called "shame-based."

2   Alice Miller, author of *The Drama of the Gifted Child* and other books relevant to the topic speaks of the many reasons childrearing practices of the past have called for children to figure out ways to stay alive and intact.

3   Refers to a TED talk by James B. Glattfelder on February 13, 2013. http://video.ted.com/talk/podcast/2012X/None/JamesBGlattfelder_2012X.mp4

4   For more information and examples of discounting, refer to chapter 22, entitled "Stop the Many Ways of Discounting" in *Growing Up Again*, Hazelden Publishing, 1998.

5   Erik Erikson created a durable model of the stages of psychosocial development. The primary focus of the second stage relates to resolving the Shame vs. Doubt dilemma. See *Identity and the Life Cycle*, W.W. Norton, 1994.

6   In 1980, after I heard Dr. Marilyn Mason's lecture, I began studying *Shame: The Power of Caring*, by Gershen Kaufman. Now in its revised and expanded third edition, it remains relevant for anyone interested

in applying the theoretical foundations of shame to the practice of psychotherapy and to the adventure of living.

7   See Appendix B.

8   More about helpful nurture may be found in Chapters 3 through 7 in *Growing Up Again*, Jean Illsley Clarke and Connie Dawson. Hazelden, 1998. Information about helpful structure may be found in Chapters 8 through 15.

9   Eric Berne identified three human hungers. *Recognition* is the hunger to be acknowledged. *Stimulation* is the hunger for the contact and movement that is vital to life. *Certainty* is the hunger for physical, social and psychological systems that keep us safe and make life predictable.

10 Pema Chodron teaches the practice of Tonglen, one way to change a tendency to make judgments of others into a practice of clearing our own. Her book *Tonglen, The Path of Transformation,* is helpful for those who want to develop this practice. http://www.shambhala.org/teachers/pema/tonglen1.php

11 Credit to Cheryl Beardsley for teaching me this strategy.

12 The work of Marshall Rosenberg is a place to begin understanding the qualities inherent in nonviolent conflict resolution. Many other authors who write about relationships offer the reader further information.

13 From a personal communication.

14 There are any number of excellent resources relating to communication to enhance intimacy. For starters, I would suggest: John M. and Julie Gottman, *The Seven Principles for Making Marriage Work, Marriage Rules, The Dance of Anger* and other books by Harriet Lerner.

15 *Forgive for Good: A Proven Prescription for Health and Happiness*, by Frederic Luskin, Ph.D. Gratitude to Monajo and Orval Ellsworth for information on Luskin's work at The Stanford Forgiveness Project.

16 An article in Whole Living www.wholeliving.com, October 2011, fleshes out the value in shifting tone instead of pointing fingers. They offer three strategies for changing things up. Step 1: Avoid the accusatory question and state the facts. Step 2: Empathize rather than criticize, and Step 3: Make your request without the negative tone.

17 In Ueland's autobiography titled *Me*, published in 1938.

18 See *Liespotting: Proven Techniques to Detect Deception*, 2011.

19   These "symptons" of criticism were identified by Jean Illsley Clarke in her self-published book titled *Ouch, That Hurts!* More about the markers of criticism will also be found in *Growing Up Again,* Hazelden, 1998.

20   Jean Illsley Clarke has a series of exercises she developed for classes for parents based on her book *Self-Esteem, A Family Affair.* Grounded in Transactional Analysis theory, each exercise teaches how to say what you mean and thereby, be able to stand by what you say.

21   From *The Synonym Finder,* Rodale Press, 1978.

22   Credit to Foster Cline, M.D. and others for identifying this way of understanding the process of developing trust or mistrust in the first several years of life.

23   Bowlby's book, *Attachment,* lays down his original theory on the caregiver-infant bond and suggests the ramifications in later life. Reading *Secure Base: Parent-Child Attachment and Healthy Human Development,* published in 1988 is a good place to start. Readers may find *Becoming Attached: Unfolding the Mystery of the Infant-Mother Bond and Its Impact on Later Life* by Robert Karen, Warner Books, 1994, a friendly and detailed story of attachment to their liking.

24   Diana Baumrind's parenting styles are presented in *Parenting for Character: Five Experts, Five Practices* by Diana Baumrind, et al.

25   This title is suggested by the title of William Stafford's poem "Every War Has Two Losers."

26   According to a study by Dana Carney, Andy J. Yap, Brian J. Lucas & Pranjal H. Mehta of Columbia University. Title: *People with Power are Better Liars.* An article by Leanne ten Brinke and Daynea Stimson titled "Some Evidence for Unconscious Lie Detection" appeared in Psychological Science, May, 2014.

27   After a book about families titled *Haven in a Heartless World* by Christopher Lasch.

28   Mellen-Thomas Benedict in *Journey Through the Light and Back.*

29   *The Divided Self* (1965) and other books by R.D. Laing speak of growing up in a family where reality was seriously contorted.

30   Derrick Jensen in *A Language Older Than Words,* Context Books, New York, 2000.

31   In *Cathexis Reader,* Harper and Row, 1975, by Jacqui Lee Schiff, she

writes: "Discounting is an internal mechanism which involves people minimizing or ignoring some aspect of themselves, others, or the reality of the situation."

32 These chapters in *Growing Up Again* contain a number of examples which illustrate the levels of discounting (denial) using everyday examples.

33 Many have described the process of integrating an unfamiliar behavior into our personal operational paradigm, among them, Virginia Satir and Gordon Training International.

34 This statement was put forward by M. Scott Peck in a lecture some twenty-odd years ago.

ACKNOWLEDGEMENTS

GRATITUDE to all sorts of other people's work, especially to Marilyn Mason, Merle Fossum and Gershen Kaufman, whose understandings of shame have been a primary motivation in exploring and changing out the rules for myself.

I am...

GRATEFUL for my experiences, both personal and professional, and for clients, students, workshop participants and friends.

GRATEFUL for these good and skillful peoples' realities and editing support:

Enid Braun, Jean Illsley Clarke, Melinda Creed, Jill Kelly, Barbara Joy Laffey, Maggie Lawrence, Deb Lund, Marsha Meyers, and A. Myrth Ogilvie.

GRATEFUL for Colleagues, past and present:

Beverly Cuevas and Tom Gill, Gary Bowman and Wayne Raiter, Scott Edelstein, Sherrie Eldridge, Joseph LeRoy and the therapists at *Hope Sparks*, Dennis Thoennes and numerous attachment theorists, researchers and attachment-oriented therapists.

GRATEFUL to my writing group:

Sherryl Christie, Barbara Joy Laffey, Deb Lund and Paula Pugh.

GRATEFUL to the many who contributed their personal stories, some included in the book, all of whom increased my understanding of the many manifestations of shame in relationships.

GRATEFUL for encouragement and tolerance:

Carol Carper, Nancy Parsons Craft, Monajo and Orval Ellsworth, Carole Gesme, Kay Lagerquist, Jane Klassen, Anne Marie McNamara, JoAnn Norman, Rose Ireland O'Brien, Mary Paananen, Beverly Rose, Marilyn Sackariason, Jean Scott, Barbara Schiltz, Joan Todd, Karin Watson, Theo Wells and Anne Glenn White

GRATEFUL TO my children, their spouses, and grandchildren who will always be my learning laboratory.

And perhaps most of all, thanks to the posse I've kept in the dark since our one and only meeting eight years ago. Your witness of my intention to work on this project made backing out impossible.